ON THE
BANKS OF
BEAUTIFUL
SAUGENAH

BOOK I of the series
Building a Michigan Lumber Town

By

Roselynn Ederer

Published by Thomastown Publishing Co., P.O. Box 6471, Saginaw, MI 48608-6471. Additional copies and volume discounts available. E-mail: Ttpublishing@aol.com

Publisher's Cataloging-in-Publication Data
Ederer, Roselynn
   On the banks of beautiful saugenah/Roselynn Ederer
   Saginaw, Mich., Thomastown Publishing Co., 1999
        p.   cm.   ill.
     ISBN 0-9664610-3-7   JUN 5 - 2002
     1. History–United States.

PROJECT COORDINATION BY BOOKABILITY, INC.

02   01   00   ◆   6   5   4   3   2   1

Printed in the United States of America

In Memory of my Grandmother

Helena Marie Schultz Ederer

1865 – 1960

FOREWORD

As a member of one of Saginaw's old line pioneering families, Rose Ederer has always had an appreciation for and an interest in the history of the area. She is a very active member of our Historical Society of Saginaw County and for many years has been our most active researcher. Thus, it is with great pleasure that we accepted her offer to research, write, and acquire photographs to provide an insert article for our society newsletter, *The Courier*.

For several years we have been delighted with these monthly transcripts of sections on our history of the Saginaw Valley. With this publication, Rose is using many of those articles as a source of material to develop a very comprehensive book dedicated to understanding our past.

We salute Rose Ederer for the tremendous effort she has put into the development of this work. The reader will find it well written with a style that makes it easy to read and I trust more enjoyable for many to learn about and appreciate the great history of Saginaw.

Charles Hoover
Executive Director
Historical Society of Saginaw County, Inc.

INTRODUCTION

Grandma provided that link to my great-grandparents, my Saginaw pioneer ancestors, all of whom gave up their Fatherland in Bavaria, Germany to create new, permanent lives for themselves and their descendants in the Saginaw Wilderness. Her numerous stories recounting her family's life in the 1800's and turn-of-the-century, told so often during my childhood, have remained dormant on my mind for decades. However, it was the rediscovery in 1988 of Grandma's collection of turn-of-the-century Saginaw postcards, which I had viewed so often as a child, that prompted me to research and write about the life that these early Saginaw pioneers lived, worked, and played while building their lumber town in the wilderness.

All eight of my great-grandparents and my grandmother left Bavaria, Germany and came to the Saginaw Wilderness to seek out a new life. My four maternal great-grandparents—the Frank and Lutz families—came in 1852 and 1853 as the founding group of St. John's Lutheran missionary colony in Amelith. My paternal great-grandparents, Wolfgang and Mary Ederer, came to Saginaw City in 1855. Wolfgang, an accomplished carpenter, built several houses in Saginaw City and the western townships. He became a founding father of James Township, helping to organize the township, after purchasing his farm there in 1866. John and Wilhelmina Schultz and their five children, which included my two-year-old grandmother, came in 1867 because John did not wish their only son, sixteen-year-old August, to serve in the German Army. The family settled on a farm in Thomastown.

Since 1989, I have been researching and writing articles about the life in the Saginaw Valley from the mid-1800's to the 1910's. Several of these articles have been published in the Saginaw County Historical Society's monthly newsletter, *The Courier.* My project started by writing stories centered about the early Saginaw postcards. Then it developed into a much broader comprehensive history of the life of these early pioneers during this era. Although the setting is the Saginaw Wilderness, this history could have taken place in several Midwestern cities in the great Northwest Territory during the same era. I am presenting my large volume of research material in a series of books, **BUILDING A MICHIGAN LUMBER TOWN.** This first book in the series, *ON THE BANKS OF BEAUTIFUL SAUGENAH,* discusses the large wave of immigration, especially the Germans and Irish, to the Saginaw Wilderness. The natural resources which brought these new settlers to the Valley were also some of the same resources that brought large numbers of settlers to other counties in Michigan and states in the Northwest Territory.

Also, I would like to acknowledge and thank those many people who have helped and encouraged me in continuing my research and writing. Nancy Krause inspired me with the idea of writing stories about the postcards. Chuck Hoover of the Historical Society published my many articles in *The Courier.* The Hoyt Public Library contains a wealth of material on Saginaw history. I spent many hours in the Eddy Historical Collection poring through books, microfilm, and other materials from the 1800's to 1910's. I could not have done this without the helpful assistance of the many librarians, especially Anna Mae Maday. The Saginaw Valley Writers Club kept me inspired, encouraged, and on track. Mary Lou Ederer has helped with the photography and given advice and assistance along the way. Michael Slasinski has graciously furnished me with photographs on the logging industry from his Great Lakes Logging & Indian Culture Museum. Talented artist Marie Walter has created the beautiful cover and the delightful illustrations on each section page. And all those many readers who kept reading my *Courier* articles, eagerly waiting for the next one, giving feedback, writing notes, and calling kept me encouraged to continue on with my project. Tom Vranich of Bookability, Inc. handled all the publishing details so this attractive book could be printed.

The illustrations in this book are from my own private collection, from the Eddy Historical Collection, and from Michael Slasinski.

It is my sincere wish that you also will enjoy reading and learning about this fascinating era of Saginaw's history as much as I have enjoyed learning and researching it.

— *Roselynn Ederer*

TABLE OF CONTENTS

PART I
THE SAGINAW WILDERNESS

Only the Indians and wildlife successfully inhabited the Saginaw Wilderness, a mosquito-infested swamp. Many potential settlers became discouraged and left. When the German missionary colonies proved the wilderness could be conquered, recruitment efforts for more Bavarian German immigrants were undertaken.

I EARLY SAGINAW DESCRIPTIONS

For centuries the *Saug-e-nah* Wilderness was a peaceful, beautiful country inhabited by the American Indians. There was an abundance of wild game and fish—pickerel, muscalonge, catfish. The rich alluvial bottom land was ideal for raising corn. Wild rice bent over the many streams and marshes. Wild nuts and fruits—walnuts, beechnuts, butternuts, hazelnuts, hickory nuts, plums, many berries, cherries, cranberries, and blackberries—grew in profusion everywhere. Maple sugar trees provided sweet delicacies. The abundant wild or pin potato provided a staple food. Blackbirds and Indians harvested the bountiful crops.

The beautiful *Saug-e-nah* Wilderness was admired by the Chippewa or Ojibwa Indians living far to the North. About 1650 they joined the Ottawa Indians who were living in the Lower Saginaw area and moved into vacant villages along the Saginaw, Shiawassee, and Tittabawassee Rivers.

The first white men to penetrate the Saginaw Wilderness were the *coureurs de bois* explorers and the French Canadian voyageurs sent by the Government. They readily assimilated the Indian life, manners and customs, paddling into the Saginaw River on their trading expeditions.

The housing for the Saginaw Valley Indians was made of birch bark as shown in this replica on display at the Saginaw Historical Museum. The bark could be packed up and moved to a new location quite easily. Also shown are some of the baskets made and used by the Chippewa Indians.

Jacob Smith may have been the first trader to come to the Wilderness in 1810. He befriended the Chippewas and urged them to be peaceful with the white men. But it was Louis Campau who came in 1816 and established a trading post on the Saginaw River at the foot of present-day Cass Street. His post was moved to Throop Street in 1822 when the Infantry arrived.

When the Chippewas became restless in 1822, the United States Government sent its Third United States Infantry into the Michigan Indian Territory. A stockade under the command of Major Daniel Baker was erected on the west bank of the river near the foot of present-day Court Street. But the floods, mosquitoes, and ague, not the Indians, drove part of the Infantry away in 1823. The remaining detachment left permanently in 1825.

In 1824 the American Fur Company established a trading post. These fur traders, the French voyageurs, and the Indians constituted the Saginaw population until about 1836. In order to keep out settlers who would spoil the excellent hunting, they always represented the Valley as cold, unhealthy, and nearly all swamp or wet prairies. Those few travelers who came by water found the land along the river generally low with wet prairies extending into the rear for miles with only occasional stands of timber. Government surveyors confirmed these unfavorable reports without actually surveying the country. They reported that the entire Valley was divided into windfalls, black ash swamps, marshes, lakes, and crooked streams. Settlers stayed away.[1]

When the French statesman, Alexis de Tocqueville visited in 1831, his guide had convinced him that the Saginaw Wilderness was "the last inhabited spot towards the Pacific." Its forest was full of Indians, mosquitoes, and ague. Yet he insisted upon coming. Departing from Pontiac, de Tocqueville and two Indian guides walked and rode on a horse through dense, unbroken forests until they penetrated the primeval forest of the Saginaw. Upon their arrival at the Saginaw Village which was actually near Green Point, they were welcomed by surveyor Eleazer Jewett and fur trader Gardner D. Williams. Scattered about were small cultivated plots, wigwams, and huts where the thirty residents had settled. The unbroken dense, dark forest stretched in all directions around them. De Tocqueville dined and slept in Jewett's cabin that evening.

As he was to write later in his *Democracy in America,* de Tocqueville wrote "In a few years these impenetrable forests will have fallen; the sons of civilization and industry will break the silence on the Saginaw;

its echoes will cease; the banks will be imprisoned with quays; its current which now flows on unnoticed and tranquil through a nameless waste, will be stemmed by great European settlements, and we were perhaps the last travellers allowed to see its primitive grandeur."[2]

Norman Little had come to Saginaw to live permanently in the 1830's. In 1836 he commissioned Harvey Williams to build a sawmill, dwelling, boarding house, barn, and blacksmith shop on the present-day City Hall site for the Mackie, Oakley & Jennison Co. of New York. Curtis Emerson and Charles W. Grant came from Detroit in 1846, purchased this sawmill, rebuilt it, then shipped clear cork pine to Albany, New York in 1847. Saginaw's lumber industry was born!

This replica of Frankenmuth's first community house which later served as the church, missionary school, and parsonage was built in 1845. It is an excellent example of the housing those early Saginaw pioneers constructed and lived in until the lumber industry got underway.

Until 1850 East Saginaw remained a dense wilderness. Only a hut or two occupied by trappers and Indians were standing in the thick impenetrable forest. The primeval forest kept out the sunlight. Salina, located only three miles south, did not have a solitary building. An Indian camp was the only vestige of human life. The primeval forest reached the river's very edge and reflected in its surface. Water courses were choked with logs and brush. The waters from the streams only slowly found their way into principal rivers, leaving much of the ground wet and flooded, unhealthy with fever and ague epidemics. There was no highway to Flint or Detroit. The Saginaw River provided the only means of transportation into the Valley. Rough cabins of the lone inhabitants were scattered about on the west bank of the river in Saginaw City. This ground was higher and drier than that in East Saginaw. In 1850 a large area in East Saginaw was cleared of its forest and eight rough buildings and a sawmill were erected. The following year population flowed in rapidly.[3]

SITE OF PRESENT CITY HALL, 1849

Curtis Emerson and Charles W. Grant rebuilt the Williams sawmill in 1846, then shipped the first cork pine to New York from this mill. This was the beginning of the Saginaw lumber industry.

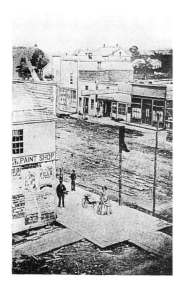

As the lumber industry got underway, white pine planks were being used to construct and improve sidewalks and muddy streets and roads.

A remarkable improvement had occurred in East Saginaw by 1853. The town now extended one and a half miles along the river. The river was dotted with one of the finest flouring mills in the West and several saw mills. A half dozen well-stocked stores, boarding houses, and many smaller establishments lined the mucky, tree-stumped streets. Public places were teeming with activity. On the river, brigs, barks, schooners, and steamboats could be seen at all hours, bringing merchandise and machinery to the wharves, or loading, then departing with Saginaw lumber to New York, Albany, Buffalo, Cleveland, Detroit, and Chicago. A steamboat now ran twice a week to Detroit loaded with Saginaw freight but returning with its decks crowded with passengers, many of them being European immigrants. Carpenters were busy building houses. The new Post Office handled a large volume of daily mail brought by stage coach from Flint. The modern telegraph connected this small wilderness town with the entire world. It was also connected to Flint by the Genesee Plank Road and from there to Detroit by the Railroad. Population had now increased to about one thousand.[4]

The Plank Road to the upper ferry was an important necessity for the town folks. Because there were no sidewalks, ladies walked in the middle of the streets during wet times. Washington Street was in the process of being planked up to Emerson's sawmill. If the stumps would be removed from the roadway, a good turnpike road put through, and two good sidewalks planked, the town would be greatly enhanced. Only one planked street through the town was sufficient for business. Planks were only thrown away where heavy teaming was done. One could not go out in the streets after dark without risk of breaking his neck over the stumps.[5]

Jesse Hoyt had purchased twenty four hundred acres in East Saginaw and with Norman Little had been steadily developing a town. Through their generosity and efforts, East Saginaw was soon destined to become one of Michigan's most prominent cities and the county one of the richest farming districts in the West. In October, 1853 the successful German Lutheran colony in Frankenmuth had applied to be organized into a township. The industrious Germans had already cleared five hundred acres. Frankenmuth Township was destined to become the most prosperous in the county.[6]

There were now three towns—East Saginaw, Saginaw City, and Lower Saginaw. Lower Saginaw was a thrifty village located on the Saginaw River about four miles from the Bay. Its high bank extended abruptly for some distance along the river. At the village's lower end, the river gently curved eastward, through low land prairies, winding its noiseless way to mingle its clear waters with those of the Huron. The partially timbered banks brought considerable lumbering and employment to the growing village. Its dozen steam mills were kept in constant operation. There were already eight hundred inhabitants and its population kept steadily increasing.[7]

The Genesee Plank Road to Flint opened up further communication with the South. Communication with Lower Saginaw was only by river. It was always difficult during the winter months until ice would break up on the Saginaw River. Plans for the Lapeer & Lower Saginaw Plank Road were already underway. When completed, this new road would bring the entire Saginaw River business in direct communication with the rich farming counties of Tuscola and Lapeer. The railroad would soon bring the entire Valley in communication with Pt. Huron and from there to Niagara Falls and New York.

The Saginaw Valley provided many attractions. Sometimes Indian Summer lasted until mid-December. Then there would be sixty days of glorious sleighing in the mild, bracing air. On several occasions deer, bear, and other wild game visited the town, taking refuge under the wharf. Saginaw's reputation of being very unhealthy had resulted during wet, flooded periods. This incorrect impression had done an injustice to the entire Valley. Actually there were very few healthy places anywhere in the country. One could hardly go south of the Mason & Dixon Line without experiencing a "shake." Consumption was seldom known in Saginaw. Ague usually occurred for a couple months in the fall but yielded readily to medical treatment.[8]

In 1859 the Government sent out a new survey team. New reports indicated the Saginaw Valley to be well timbered with rich soil. The Cass, Shiawassee, Bad, and Tittabawassee Rivers fed by the Pine, Tobacco, and numerous small streams joined at Green Point to form the twenty-five mile long Saginaw River. This river was navigable for twenty-four miles. The rivers emptying into the Saginaw drained hundreds of miles of country rich in timber and soil. Land bordering the rivers was timbered with oak, beech, maple, basswood, ash, butternut, black walnut, and hickory. The soils were rich, muddy, gravelly logans. Crops grown in New York—winter wheat, corn, oats, pasture grazing—also grew well here. The Valley climate was mild, seldom extremely cold, and the country was healthy. In the previous eight years the snow had never been more than twenty inches deep during the winter season. Fruits of all kinds—apples, pears, peaches, plums—grew in abundance.

The Tittabawassee River, about the size of the Merrimack River, was the most beautiful little river out West. It was navigable all the way to Midland City and provided the great avenue for log transportation from Michigan's northern interior. Logs were brought one hundred twenty-five miles on the Tittabawassee, seventy-five miles on the Chippewa and Pine, twenty-five miles on the Tobacco, Molasses, Salt, and Little Salt Rivers. In the 1858 lumber season, sixty five million feet of logs were brought to the Saginaw River along these waterways. In 1859, one hundred twenty million feet were expected. Lumber camps were rapidly being erected along the waterways. Artesian wells were being sunk along the Saginaw River to bore for salt in East Saginaw. Michigan was soon destined to become the wealthiest state of the entire West.

New buildings were being erected throughout Saginaw City in 1859. Water Street from Emerson's Ferry to Lyon Street, a distance of one and a half miles, was being planked. Court and Mackinaw Streets and two other streets from the river to the city limits were graded. A grist mill at the foot of Mackinaw Street adjoining the ferry landing was under construction. The Methodist Society was building a chapel. The German Lutheran Society had just enlarged its building and built a steeple. First-class residences were being built all over the city. Newell Barnard had just erected his palatial residence at Throop and Hamilton

Streets. Moderate dwellings were being constructed in the suburbs. Additional housing was needed for the rapidly increasing population, many being European immigrants.[9]

The Bancroft House had opened in September, 1859 in East Saginaw under Proprietor Hobbs' management. The House was more like a first-class hotel in New York instead of one in the wilderness. Mr. Hobbs showed all his guests the hospitalities of a large city inside the House and those of the wilderness outside. A deer, bear, or other wild game could be easily shot just outside its doors a short distance away, then served up in grand style to the guests.

By 1865 the Flint & Holly and Flint & Pere Marquette Railroads were some of the best in Michigan. They daily brought traffic into the Saginaws. The Saginaws now had eleven thousand inhabitants. There were magnificent hotels, stores and public buildings. The maritime commerce had enlarged so that sails lined and whitened the entire river border. Where the Indian fleetly followed the river trail only a short time ago, a splendid street railway now stretched its iron length. Splendid steamers now were moored on the same spot where in 1850 the Indian secured his dug-out by its bark fastening. The whole scene was so marvelously changed that one could not recognize it as the same place only fifteen years ago. Brick, mortar, lumber and salt had become a reality. The street railway ran several times daily from the Bancroft House at the foot of Washington Street to Salina three miles away. The street railways enhanced property values. Streets were laid out and numerous houses had been erected.[10]

The day would soon come when both Cities would be linked together as one. There was no other place in the state with such immense resources. The quantity of lumber, staves, and salt manufactured here must be seen to be fully comprehended. Mere figures did not convey the true picture of the lumber piles and seas of salt barrels existing all along the river. In another twenty years the Saginaws would equal or surpass Detroit in resources, size, and manufacturing. Men of enterprise had invested their capital in land, lumber, and public buildings. Money was plentiful. With interest of two per cent per month any enterprising individual could borrow enough to operate a lumber camp and make his fortune. Several societies, schools, churches, and homes were being built as substantial and beautiful edifices.

This Holy Cross Lutheran school and teacherage were built on Hermansau Street in Saginaw City in 1861. With the expansion of the lumber industry, the congregation had outgrown their old school. This property later became Bethlehem Lutheran Church. These buildings are representative of the type of construction replacing the first log cabins of the early settlers. Lumber was now plentiful. Wooden fences were built around yards to keep horses and livestock enclosed and strays from entering. Streets were muddy, low spots with water pockets most of the time.

By 1870 any traveler wishing to see Michigan needed to visit Saginaw. The countryside was flat and monotonous. From Flint to Saginaw the Railroad ran through timbered land. East Saginaw was a great city with handsome brick stores and dwellings. The Bancroft House carried Saginaw's fame far and wide. Here merchants, ship owners, lumber dealers and travelers congregated and conducted their business. The river banks were a continuous scene of bustling activity. There were piles of lumber as far as the eye reached, white mills and tall chimneys sending forth volumes of smoke, continuous docks, rafts of logs, tugs, steamboats and ferryboats continually on the move. Lumber and its debris were everywhere. Docks were made with refuse slabs. Large areas of low, wet ground were now filled in with sawdust and refuse from the sawmills. Everywhere there were handsome suburban residences, many Nicholson-paved streets, well-stocked stores. Lumber and salt gave the lasting impression of permanent, solid prosperity.[11]

Alexis de Tocqueville's prophecy was already fulfilled. Only twenty years previous Saginaw City had barely five hundred inhabitants and East Saginaw was still a dense wilderness. There hardly existed any mark of civilization. The rapid advancement had greatly changed the town. The past had almost been forgotten in the present. The thousands of Indians who held their headquarters in East Saginaw twenty years ago now lived in scattered housing. A solitary Indian on the streets today attracted much attention. Plank roads stretching around the Saginaws made farming country accessible to the City. Norman Little and Jesse Hoyt were instrumental in helping East Saginaw achieve its greatness.

By 1884 East Saginaw with its population of thirty thousand and Saginaw City with fifteen thousand took the lead as the second city in Michigan. East Saginaw was the geographical center of the state. Its commercial advantages and lake navigation gave the Cities additional advantages. Lake vessels could land at the docks. The principal streams and rivers in Michigan's interior were tributaries of the Saginaw. As timber land was being cleared, fine agricultural land, more productive than that out West, was being put into cultivation. The Saginaws had now become a great industrial center with two flouring mills, thirteen planing mills, salt blocks, several small wagon and carriage factories, stave mills, a furniture factory, thirteen iron industries, and many other successful enterprises. Lumber shipments ranged up to one hundred thousand car loads yearly. The Saginaws were truly the hub of commerce and activity, second only to Detroit.

FOOTNOTES

1 *East Saginaw Courier*, June 16, 1859

2 Mills, *History of Saginaw County*, page 78

3 *East Saginaw Courier*, September 6, 1865

4 *Saginaw Weekly Enterprise*, September 15, 1853

5 *Ibid*

6 *Saginaw Enterprise*, October 20, 1853

7 *Saginaw Weekly Enterprise*, September 29, 1853

8 *East Saginaw Courier*, June 16, 1859

9 *East Saginaw Courier*, August 18, 1859

10 *Ibid*, September 6, 1865

11 *Saginaw Daily Courier*, October 26, 1870

BIBLIOGRAPHY

Mills, James, *History of Saginaw County*, Volume I, 1918, pages 1 – 96

East Saginaw Courier,
June 16, 1859, page 2;
August 18, 1859, page 3;
December 15, 1859, page 1;
July 19, 1860, page 3;
September 6, 1865, page 2

Saginaw Courier Herald,
August 2, 1903, page 9;
August 18, 1907;
October 13, 1910

Saginaw Daily Courier,
March 18, 1869, page l;
May 9, 1870, page 2;
September 7, 1870, page 4;
October 26, 1870, page 2;
December 14, 1884, page l

Saginaw Enterprise,
September 15, 1853, page 3;
October 20, 1853, page 2;
January 5, 1854, page 3;
February 16, 1854, page 2

Saginaw Evening News, July 22, 1887, page 6

Saginaw Weekly Enterprise,
September 15, 1853, page 2;
September 29, 1853, page 2;
March 1, 1854, page 2;
November 16, 1865, page 3;
January 18, 1866, page 3;
June 18, 1868, page 4

II THE FOUR GERMAN MISSIONARY COLONIES

Many newly-arriving German immigrants found their way to the Northwest Territory's wilderness during the 1830's. These immigrants lived in scattered, isolated settlements, which they had cleared, with little communication with each other. Lutheran missionary Friedrich Conrad Dietrich Wyneken came from Hanover, Germany to Baltimore in 1838. He spent the next several years ministering to these German immigrants' spiritual needs in Indiana, Ohio, and southern Michigan. The itinerant missionary treked on horseback from his Fort Wayne headquarters to their many scattered settlements, preaching the gospel to small groups and baptizing children whose parents were gradually falling away from the German Protestant church. No Lutheran churches existed in the wilderness.

Each year brought an ever increasing number of German immigrants migrating westward to seek out a new life. There were very few German Lutheran ministers available to minister to these immigrants' spiritual needs. In Ohio there were Andrew and Charles Henkel; in Michigan Friedrich Schmidt. Wyneken realized that if all the German Protestant immigrants might be brought together, the Lutheran Church could be the largest Protestant denomination in the

United States. In 1840 he sent out written appeals or *Notruf* to Germany pleading for more American missionary help. Groups formed in Bremen and Stade to assist in this missionary appeal. Appeals were made in the *Sonntagblatt,* the most widely read publication in Franconia. Several Germans responded by sending money for the missionary cause. Also, many young men indicated an interest in going to America as missionaries.[1]

It was Reverend Johann Konrad Wilhelm Loehe, the young pastor in the little village of Neudettelsau, Franconia, Germany, who became profoundly interested in this missionary cause. He began recruiting and preparing young men for missionary work in the Northwest Territory. Through his direction and recruitment, he helped to found Frankenmuth and several German Lutheran colonies in the Saginaw Valley and became the greatest benefactor of Lutheranism in the Midwest.[2]

Lorenz Loesel, influenced by Wyneken's appeal, became interested in doing missionary work with the Chippewa Indians. He persuaded Loehe to establish a missionary colony in Michigan. Loehe recruited Reverend Friedrich August Craemer, a new graduate of Erlangen University, and thirteen colonists, including Loesel. This small group planned to leave Germany in the spring of 1845 and settle on the Cass River in Michigan, specifically in the Saginaw Wilderness. Throughout the winter of 1844, the group met on Saturday evenings and Sundays, discussing their new colony, studying doctrine, and learning hymns, the Lutheran liturgy and constitution. Loehe's plan was to Christianize the Indians by establishing a colony so the Indians could learn about life in a Christian community.[3]

Germany's Foreign Mission Society provided the funds for

establishing this new Michigan colony. Loehe contacted Reverend Friedrich Schmidt, the Lutheran missionary in Ann Arbor and Monroe. Both Schmidt and Reverend J.J. Auch, the missionary in Sebewaing, had selected a site for the colony on the Cass River, about fifteen miles upstream from Upper Saginaw. The colony was to be named Frankenmuth, meaning *Courage of the Franconians.*

The missionary group departed Bremen, Germany on April 20, 1845 on the ship *Caroline.* In addition to their personal belongings, the colonists took a large painting of the crucifixion, two church bells, altar crucifix, pulpit Bible, cathechism, hymnbook, communion vessels, their own bedding, cooking utensils and some food supplies. When their ship became stuck in a sandbank just outside Bremen, Reverend Craemer married the four betrothed couples who had intended to marry upon leaving Germany. Because they lacked the resources required by German law, they could not marry in Germany.

There were seventy total passengers on this ship, many very boisterous, who ridiculed the missionary group. The colonists purchased an accordian on shipboard and used it during their morning and evening devotions while the other passengers played accordians for their singing and dancing pastimes. The passengers encountered pleasant sailing days and storms at sea, seasickness, and smallpox. A two-year old child of the colonists died of smallpox before reaching New York. Craemer had met and fallen in love with another passenger, Dorothea Benthien, a single unmarried mother traveling with her five-year-old son. The ship arrived in New York harbor on June 8. Reverend Craemer and Dorothea were married in New York. Their marriage remained a contention with the colonists for months afterwards.

On June 12 the missionary group of fifteen Bavarian men and women left New York on the steamer, *Knickerbocker,* traveling to Albany. Then as they traveled by railroad to Buffalo while singing the hymn *Now Thank We All Our God,* their train was wrecked, but none of their group was injured. They continued by steamboat on Lake Erie to Monroe, Michigan. Here they were welcomed by members of the Lutheran colony in Monroe.

These German immigrants first began adopting American ways when the women shed their woolen Bavarian bonnets for the cooler, wide-brimmed straw hats. On June 27, they resumed their journey by steamboat to Detroit, where Reverend Schmidt met them. They left their three thousand dollars in gold pieces with Reverend Winkler's Lutheran congregation in Detroit. From Detroit they traveled by railroad to Pontiac, where they then boarded the sailing vessel *Nelson Smith* propelled by Captain Munson on July 3.

Upon awakening the following morning, the colonists were frightened to hear shooting and explosions; they thought a war was nearby. Instead, it was the Fourth of July! While Captain Munson and his crew left the ship to partake in the day's festivities, the colonists remained on board the ship all day in the scorching heat. After a week of sailing, the *Nelson Smith* arrived at Lower Saginaw. There was no wind to push the vessel up the Saginaw River. Not wishing to wait longer for favorable sailing, the colonists, weary from the heat, travel, and mosquitoes, pulled the sailing vessel by ropes like a canal boat up the Saginaw River all the way to Saginaw City. When they finally arrived on July 10, Reverend Auch met the group. He had already rented a large house for them in Saginaw City.[4]

Using maps, Craemer, Auch, a surveyor, and the missionary men broke their way through the primeval forests until they reached the designated sections they wished to purchase, fifteen miles inland from the Saginaw River on the Cass River. Bridgeport was about five miles away. They purchased six hundred eighty acres on the Indian Reservation site at two dollars fifty cents per acre for a total of seventeen hundred dollars. Seventy acres were set aside for the church-parsonage-school. Reverend Auch returned to Detroit to retrieve the gold pieces. He carried the three thousand dollars in a wooden bucket to the Land Office in Flint.

The men spent July and August clearing the land and building a single log cabin and a church-parsonage-school. The two church

These two church bells were cast in Nuremberg, Germany and brought with the first Frankenmuth settlers on the Caroline. These bells were hung in the first church parsonage-school and rung on December 25, 1845. Each missionary colony used bells in its church. The bells called the congregation together for worship since there were no clocks. These bells still stand today in Frankenmuth.

bells were hung in this building on Christmas Day. The other twelve members of the group moved to Frankenmuth on August 18, 1845 and lived a communal life in their single log cabin until the spring of 1846 when they were able to build their individual log cabins on their own scattered farms.

In June, 1846 another ninety Bavarian men, women, and children arrived in Frankenmuth. They were the founders and builders of Frankenmuth as well as the leaders in the development of St. Lorenz Lutheran Church. They laid out their new village like their Bavarian German villages they had left behind.

While the settlers were building their houses, clearing the land, farming, establishing a mill and their town, Reverend Craemer carried on his missionary work with the Chippewa Indians. His work was done with interpreters, the French-Catholic Tromble and the

Each missionary colony had its own cemetery next to the church. These markers designate the grave sites of those first settlers to Frankenmuth. The church-school parsonage replica is in the background.

Canadian-French half-breed Indian, James Gruet. He often traveled to their tents, living and eating with them for several days. The Indian children lived and learned at the parsonage school. Mrs. Craemer scrubbed the Indian children, removing dirt and lice, and taught them table manners. St. Lorenz was the only place in the United States where the Indians were trilingual, learning both English and German, in addition to their own native Chippewa tongue.[5]

Reverend Craemer baptized three Indian children in 1846 and nineteen in 1848. By 1854 there were thirty-four Indian children baptized in the Lutheran church. Craemer had left Frankenmuth in 1849 and had been succeeded by Reverend K.A.W. Roebbelen in 1851. The congregation's first church was a log cabin, 42' x 26', with three windows on each side, built in 1846. When the second St. Lorenz Church, built like those in Germany, was dedicated on September 29, 1852, there were three hundred forty-five members and forty-three children. This new frame building was 74' x 40' x 74' high. The chimney and stove were installed in 1853, the organ in 1861, the balconies and chancel in 1864. Men sat on the left side and women on the right side facing the altar.

In the fall of 1846 Wilhelm Loehe planned his second colony to be named Frankentrost, meaning *Consolation of the Franconians*. Several peasants with large families applied to go to this new colony. Loehe carefully selected all his colonists. All were required to have good moral reputations. About sixty men, women, and children were scheduled to depart in the spring of 1847. Reverend Johann Heinrich Philipp Graebner was appointed as their minister. These new colonists collected and sent twenty four hundred dollars to Reverend Craemer to select a suitable site for their new colony.

Because their scheduled ship was delayed, the group split into two groups. One group left April 18, 1847 from Bremerhaven on the *Creole.* They arrived in New York on June 12. The second group left April 21, 1847 on the *Hermine,* arriving in New York on June 1. Missionary Baierlein accompanied the second group; he was sent to continue the missionary efforts with the Chippewa Indians. Both groups continued their journeys separately to Albany, Buffalo, and Detroit. From Detroit they traveled by wagons to Flint, then on to Frankenmuth. The second group arrived in Pine Run (Clio) on June 9, then in Frankenmuth on June 10. The first group arrived in Frankenmuth on June 24. The colonists in Frankenmuth celebrated both of their arrivals as holidays and took them into their own individual homes until the newcomers would be able to move into their own log cabins.

With the services of a surveyor, Craemer, Graebner, and several of the men broke through the primeval forest, selecting Sections 29, 30, 31, and 32 in what eventually became Blumfield Township. The two creeks that flowed through these sections could drain the swampy, mosquito-infested lowlands. This site was seven miles northwest of Frankenmuth and fifteen miles east of Saginaw. On July 22 they purchased this land for seventy-seven cents per acre.

Individual parcels of land were surveyed for each family. Unlike the scattered farms in Frankenmuth, their individual houses and farms extended one mile long and were built in a straight row. In the center of the parcels, ninety-six acres were reserved for the church-parsonage-school. Each family contributed the price of every twentieth acre for the support of the church. A leaf shelter was built for a community home. The men lived in this shelter while they continued to build their individual log cabins.

In October, the wives and children left Frankenmuth and moved into their new log cabins, which were rough-hewn with clay floors. The group endured many hardships, lacking both money and food. Several men found work in the sawmills. The Frankentrost colony lived an isolated existence. The footpath to Frankenmuth was quickly overgrown with brush. Wild animals roamed the dark, unbroken forest. Walking to Saginaw or Flint took several days, as one usually became lost in the forest. If one didn't return within two days, a search party went through the dense forest shouting and blowing horns, trying to find the lost soul.

Immanuel Lutheran Church was organized and immediately became a member of the Missouri Synod which was also founded in Chicago in 1847. Until a separate log cabin church was built, church services were held in the home of Conrad Munker. Pastor Graebner lived in the attic. The living room was used for Sunday church services, daily morning and evening devotions, and weekday school classes for the fifteen children. In the evening Mrs. Munker often served *Kartoffelkloesze*, and the entire group ate a common meal together. The colonists enjoyed close Christian fellowship at the Munker household. A 20' x 30' two-room cabin was built that winter. One room served as both the parsonage and school; the other was the church. The small room had an altar, a lectern, and nine pews which were rough-hewn planks laid over two large tree stumps. The church cabin had no stove, organ, or heat. Devotions were conducted here daily every morning and evening. A communion service was conducted every Sunday morning. A *Christenlehre* or Cathecism questioning was conducted throughout every Sunday afternoon.

Because there were no church bells to announce the service, Pastor Graebner blew a tin horn and each settler in turn blew his horn or called to his neighbor. As the morning sun was breaking over the tree tops, the dedicated colonists treked dutifully through the forest path to attend private confessions at the parsonage, then the morning devotion service in the church. Private confessions were held until

1872. Although the beautiful little church with its three windows was lacking many material comforts, it often was filled with the warmth, radiance, and beauty of the rising sun and the fragrance of green forest boughs.

The congregation steadily increased. In 1852 a new 28' x 40' log cabin church was built. There were one hundred sixty members by

1853 when Reverend Graebner was called to Detroit. Reverend H. Dicke of Amelith was then installed in 1854. In 1866 a new parsonage was built. In 1868 membership reached three hundred and a new 38' x 60' frame church was built. It had a 100' tower and two church bells. Balconies and an organ were added later.[6]

These colonists organized Blumfield Township on February 9, 1853. They organized and managed the township in the same way they organized and conducted their religious and daily lives.

Loehe's third colony would be named Frankenlust, meaning *Love of the Franconians*. He selected a recent university graduate, Reverend George Ernst Christian Ferdinand Sievers, to found this colony in 1847. Reverends Sievers, E.A. Brauer, and J.H. Pinkepank left Bremen on the *Florian* on August 20, 1847. The Bavarians selected for this colony left Bremen three days later. Upon arriving in New York, Sievers immediately departed for Frankenmuth. To his disappointment, the colonists never followed him. Instead, they traveled to and remained at Monroe, Frankenmuth, and Wisconsin. Founding this new colony was impossible at this time.

Sievers spent the winter looking for a suitable site for Frankenlust. He made several trips to the Tittabawassee River area but decided that the soil was too poor, swampy, and unsuitable for habitation. He purchased a six hundred-acre site eleven miles north of Saginaw on the Squaconning River.

A group of seventeen men, women, and children left Bremen on the *Regina* on April 18, 1848, arriving in New York on June 3 and in Saginaw on June 18. On June 22 the group assembled in Gerhard Dierker's barn, west of Saginaw City. Here they organized St. Paul Lutheran Church and called Reverend Sievers as their pastor. In

Dierker's barn on June 25 Sievers held the congregation's first Holy Communion service and married four betrothed couples. During the next several days the colonists cleared a six-acre parcel and planted potatoes to help sustain them through the winter.

A group of fifteen, including Pastor Sievers, departed for the Frankenlust site on July 4. They separated into two groups. With Sievers as their guide, one group treked through the primeval forest driving their cow which they had purchased. Again and again, explosions echoed through the silent forest with each cannon shot fired in Saginaw City during the Fourth of July celebration. After an exhausting trek through the dense forest, they arrived weary and hungry, at the Squaconning River bridge that evening. They had no food, dishes, utensils, or pails and could not even milk their cow. They slept on the ground and the bridge board that evening.

Meanwhile, the second group traveled down the Saginaw River on a scow towing an eighty-five-hundred foot raft of lumber to be used to build their communal shanty. They also carried three hundred fifty dollars worth of tools, stoves, windows, flour, food and household goods which had been bought in Detroit. The undaunted group laboriously, slowly pushed their scow through the tangled brush, marsh weeds, and profusely-growing wild rice at the Squaconning River, but they were unable to reach Frankenlust until July 5.

The lumber raft was used to build a shanty which was not waterproof. During the next several rainy days, the group sat inside on their boxes and trunks, holding their umbrellas. The six-hundred-acre tract was divided and sold to the colonists. Each family paid twelve and one-half cents to the church treasury for each acre purchased. A total of one hundred and four acres were set aside for the church-parsonage-school.

Hardships and typhoid epidemics plagued the colony. Both Sievers and the colonists became very ill. In spite of illness and deaths, they cleared their acreage and built their log cabins. Their first 28' x 24' log cabin church was dedicated on November 12, 1849. The altar was beautifully decorated with evergreens and autumn foliage. There were no bells, organ, painting, or pulpit. A frame building, 70' x 30'

This first frame church replaced the original log cabin church in Frankenlust in 1857 and was used until 1905. All the missionary colonies replaced their log cabin churches with a similar frame church. Lumber was plentiful.

St. Pauls-Kirche zu Frankenlust.

x 22' high, church replaced this log cabin on October 4, 1857. This church served the congregation until 1905. Sievers built the first parsonage in 1849 with the funds and specifications supplied by his future father-in-law Bergrat Friedrich Koch before he allowed his daughter to marry Sievers. Sievers owned this parsonage until his death in 1893.[7]

Instead of Christianizing the Indians, Pastor Sievers' missionary efforts extended to the neighboring communities where other German Lutheran immigrants had settled. A number of immigrants whom Loehe had selected for his colonies did not go to the planned ones but instead chose to settle in and around Saginaw City. Adam Geuder offered his blacksmith shop in Saginaw City where this group of Lutherans met and discussed the founding of another church. Paster Sievers was called to minister to them. Then, every Sunday afternoon, Sievers would walk from Frankenlust through the dense forest and swamps along the banks of the Saginaw River, a distance of eleven miles, arriving at Saginaw City in the evening to preach a Sunday service to this small Lutheran group. After his father-in-law provided the funds, he purchased a white horse. Then the group intently watched for his arrival and cheered when they saw a moving white patch against the dark green trees. Now he was able to preach the gospel on Sunday afternoons.

Postmaster Gardner D. Williams invited this group of Saginaw City Lutherans to his home on January 29, 1849. With the guidance of Pastor Sievers, Holy Cross Lutheran Church was organized. Mr. Williams would give the new church lots 7 and 8 of block 30 in southern Saginaw City and the purchase rights of another four lots. Six men signed the agreement to organize and pledged a total of one hundred and two dollars towards building a church. Since all the men were quite poverty stricken, they gave their pledges in building supplies rather than cash. Reverend Sievers declined their call to serve as the pastor since he was already committed to Frankenlust. But Reverend Ottomar Cloeter accepted the call on October 17, 1849. Church services were held in the Courthouse and in private homes until their own church would be built.

In the fall of 1850 the congregation purchased a ten acre forest tract on Mackinaw Road. In June 1851 the church purchased a lot on the southeast corner of Court & Washington (Michigan) and let a contract to Stenglein & Ganschow. A shanty of rough boards was built on the lot and used for worship until their church would be

"The Old Dutch Saltblock" was nicknamed after the many salt blocks which were already lining the Saginaw River. This building was not far from the River.

completed. On November 16, 1851 their 42' x 28' church was dedicated. The building with its unusual architecture and one hundred-fifty- pound bell in a small steeple, looked more like the many salt works which lined the Saginaw River. It was often called *the old Dutch Saltblock.* Reverend Cloeter converted the shanty into his parsonage and used it for a Christian school. A house and two lots were purchased in 1855 and used as a parsonage until 1867.

When the heirs to this church property filed a claim, the congregation repurchased the tract for four hundred fifty dollars in 1853. The church was enlarged and an organ purchased in 1853. A teacher's dwelling and a school were built on Hermansau Street in 1861. Saginaw's lumber and salt booms also influenced the

Holy Cross Lutheran Church built a parsonage, two-story school, and church in 1868. The church was dedicated on February 7, 1869 and used until torn down in 1955. The school was demolished in 1968. A new church and school stand today on the same site across from the Court House.

congregation's growth. By 1865 there were already ninety voting members. In 1866 the congregation purchased property on Court Street between Fayette & Harrison Streets for three thousand dollars. After selling the ten acres on Mackinaw Road, another two acres on Cross Road were purchased for a cemetery. The old church property was sold for eight thousand dollars. A new parsonage was built at a cost of twelve hundred dollars; a two-room school at twenty five hundred, and a new brick church at a cost of eighteen thousand dollars. The church was dedicated on February 7, 1869. Three church bells and a pipe organ were added. In twenty-five years, this unplanned *Loehe's Fifth Colony* had built two churches, five schools, and two parsonages. Daughter congregations were later established: Trinity Lutheran in East Saginaw in 1884 and Bethlehem Lutheran in 1915 on the Hermansau School property.[8]

In 1850 Loehe had planned to establish a Pilgrims' Home in Saginaw City. This Protestant monastery would serve as a shelter for newly-arriving German Lutherans, a hospital, and theological seminary. In June 1852 Director Grossmann from Hesse, Germany arrived with five pupils, who later all became teachers and ministers in the Lutheran church. Reverend Cloeter taught at this seminary. The Home was located in a rented renovated store which eventually was enlarged to a two-story frame building on Washington & Adams Streets (present day Ardern's Flower Shop). In 1853 Loehe severed ties with the Lutheran theology which he had established in the Saginaw colonies. All the Saginaw colonies had already become members of the Missouri Synod. After he separated himself from his colonies, this Home was soon disbanded. The property was sold and the seminary was moved elsewhere.[9]

Reverend Sievers had served as a tutor in the wealthy home of Bergrat Friedrich Koch before he emigrated to America. There, he had fallen in love with his daughter, Caroline Koch. In 1850 Herr Koch accompanied his daughter to Frankenlust to marry Sievers. Koch had previously provided the funds to build a suitable parsonage

Bergrat Koch of Germany supplied the funds and specifications to build this parsonage in 1849 so that his daughter Caroline could marry Reverend Sievers and have a suitable home. Sievers owned the parsonage until his death in 1893.

and home for his daughter. At the same time the Revolution of 1848 was threatening to close Koch's mines and factories in Germany. Wanting to provide for his faithful employees, Koch purchased twenty-five hundred acres of land at one dollar twenty five cents per acre from the government. He named the tract Kochville Township and the community Amelith after his wife's birthplace. He donated eighty acres for the church property. Then he provided the funds so the Frankenlust men could build a log cabin to be used as a temporary shelter and church for the new colonists.

Bergrat Koch's mines were never forced to close, so none of his

This replica of St. John's log cabin church was made for Amelith's Centennial celebration in 1952. Each missionary colony began with a log cabin church similar to this one.

employees ever came to Amelith. However, friends and relatives of the Frankenlust colony found their way to Amelith. In the fall of 1851 two families came and lived in the log cabin. In 1852 at least ten additional families came and founded St. John's Lutheran Church. In 1853 another eighteen families joined this colony. Reverend Sievers walked through the swampy, dense forest to minister to this new colony. Reverend H. Dicke served the congregation in 1853, but then a number of other pastors came and left until 1868 when Reverend J.F. Mueller accepted the call and lived in the log cabin church.

This colony was plagued by difficulties, including a lack of money and its own live-in pastor. Trading was done by barter. The

Amelith's second church was this frame church built in 1870. The church cemetery is to the rear of the church; the instructional building for Cathecism is to the right. On the left side are the long horse barns. Every family was assigned a horse stall, and was responsible for its maintenence. On Sundays the father would stop at the church door and let the mother, girls, and young children out of the buggy. Then the father and sons would unhitch the horse and buggy and put the horse in its stall to eat and drink. After the Sunday service, the father and sons would hitch up the horse and buggy, then drive to the church door for the mother and family. To the rear left is the school and parsonage.

temporary log cabin served until 1870 when a new church was built at a cost of five thousand dollars. Until 1885 each family was required to furnish up to one cord of firewood yearly for the church. Although the families themselves struggled with poverty, they never refused aid for sister congregations elsewhere in America or Germany.

By the early 1890's church membership declined. The period of expansion had ended. Farms and homes were now established all around Amelith. Many families joined Frankenlust. The family size had decreased. Then suddenly church membership increased when coal mines were established in Kochville. Amelith's population

This beautiful brick building was Amelith's third church and replaced the old frame church in October 1912. The church still stands today. All the missionary colonies built their third churches similar to this brick church, which also resembled those they had left behind in Germany.

increased. It became a village with its own post office. St. John's frame church was replaced with a beautiful brick church in October 1912. The attractive stained glass windows added charm and beauty to this obscure rural village. Other Lutheran congregations used Amelith's new church as a model when designing their own churches.

Amelith began a combination public and Lutheran school

The beautiful interior of Amelith's church reflects the German heritage of those early settlers. Its interior design is repeated in many German Lutheran churches. Sunday services were given exclusively in German until WWII. Since then both English and German services were given every Sunday. Now German services are given only on special occasions.

experiment in 1869.   During the winter months the teacher taught public school studies, mainly English and social studies.   During the remainder of the year, the same teacher taught the parochial school studies in religion, German, arithmetic, and singing. In 1875 a two-room school was built. One teacher taught the upper grades in the public school while another teacher taught the lower grades in the parochial school during the mornings. They reversed in the afternoon sessions.   Each day a student received dual training in both public and parochial schools.   This arrangement continued until 1905 when the state and county authorities discontinued it.[10]

Reverend Sievers continued his missionary work by establishing daughter congregations in Monitor, Beaver, and Mt. Pleasant in 1850, and Immanuel in Lower Saginaw in 1858. He served these colonies traveling on horseback, preaching in private homes until each congregation could call its own pastor.

Loehe's plan for his fourth colony was Frankenhilf, meaning *Aid for the Franconians.* In 1849 Reverend Sievers purchased one thousand five hundred ninety two acres on the Cheboygening River, eight miles northeast of Frankenmuth and six miles east of Frankentrost. Loehe wanted to establish a colony for poor people who had no prospects to marry in Germany. These people were required to pay their fares to America. Then each would be furnished a parcel of land and a cabin. When they couldn't work their own land, they would be given employment and from those wages they gradually could buy their own land. Loehe intended that a match factory, mills, and other businesses would be established in this colony so these people might find immediate employment.

In 1850 several families with Reverend Herman Kuehn came to America. However, they remained in Monroe, Detroit, and other settlements. Only Gottlieb Ammon and Michael Schwarz accompanied Kuehn to Frankenhilf. They cleared land and built a cabin. On August 17, Kuehn accepted a call in Illinois. In June of 1851 Reverend Johannes Deindoerfer and another four families arrived. They founded St. Michael's Lutheran Church, Richville. Several other families arrived and joined this colony in 1852 and 1853.

In only two years time twenty families had joined Frankenhilf. In 1853 Mr. Ammon donated four acres of land to the church, and the first log cabin church was built. Building materials and labor were donated by the members. Dissension was always present in this colony because it was operating under the Bavarian Society for Inner Missions rather than the Missouri Synod. At the same time Loehe had serious doctrinal differences with the Missouri Synod so he severed his relationship with both the Synod and the colonies. On September 4 the church property was formally transferred to the congregation. Both Deindoerfer and the Ammons left for Iowa and founded the Iowa Synod.

Because of their poverty, the congregation had difficulty calling and keeping ministers. The congregation experienced stability and growth when Reverend G. Bernthal arrived in 1862. Many Germans in Frankenmuth discovered the fertile soil and bought farms in Richville for their children. By 1874 membership had increased to thirty-five and a new church similar to that in Amelith was built. As membership continued increasing, the church was renovated in 1890. In a period of thirty years this poverty-stricken congregation had built a church and parsonage, four schools, four teacherages, and a confirmation house. They had set an example for other struggling colonies.[11]

German Saxons living in Missouri had organized the Missouri Synod Lutheran Church in the summer of 1847 in Chicago. As each of these Saginaw colonies organized their own Lutheran church, they soon joined the Missouri Synod. While establishing his colonies Wilhelm Loehe intended them to become a permanent part of the German Reich and government. Loehe had no conception of an American free democratic state. Germany was another world, thousands of miles away. The colonists' hardships and life were far removed from those they had left behind in their Bavarian villages. The early leaders of the Synod—Walther, Wyneken, Brohm—helped to organize Lutheran congregations that would be self-governing.

Loehe believed that the clergy should be the church's ruling power. He disapproved of these democratizing and Americanizing principles. In 1853 Loehe severed his ties with the Missouri Synod and the Saginaw colonies which he had helped to establish. However, all of these colonists became loyal citizens of Michigan and the United States. Their colonies thrived and expanded. Today all of these Lutheran churches they founded have celebrated their 150th Anniversaries.[12]

The missionary attempts with the Indians were soon disbanded. To successfully Christianize the Indians, the Lutheran missionaries needed to follow the nomadic tribes, not attempting to change them. The Methodists had been in the area since 1829, traveling with the Indians, teaching lay Indian preachers, not attempting to civilize them. Their missionary attempts were successful long after the Lutherans disbanded theirs.

Life for these early Saginaw pioneers was extremely difficult. They purchased tracts of primeval forest, cleared the land and built their cabins. They felled the mighty giants of the forest, then cut, rolled, and burned them. They endured swamps, marshes, and mosquitoes. A temporary communal cabin was erected before they built their own individual cabins. These were rough, crude, had clay floors, and often leaked. Fireplaces were used for cooking and warmth. Their tables, chairs, and beds were all handmade from the trees they felled. Money was non-existent in these isolated colonies. Bartering for food and supplies was the mode. Men worked in sawmills to earn cash. Either drought or floods often destroyed their crops. Sometimes corn bread and mushrooms were their only food. At times they had both flour and potatoes, usually not both. Acorns and beechnuts were brewed for coffee. Sugar and vinegar were made from maple sap. Venison and wild game were abundant in the dark forest. There were no roads. They treked on Indian trails through swamps and forests to Frankenmuth, Saginaw City, or Flint to purchase flour and supplies, often getting lost in the forest during the trip. Fevers, epidemics, illnesses, and deaths were common.

But these Bavarian Germans set an excellent example for the Saginaw lumber men and the State of Michigan. Pauperism was non-existent. Each colony cared for its own poor and infirm. Taxes were always paid and mortgages were non-existent. Every family owned his own home and farm. There were no lawsuits or intervention by local judges. These German peasants came to America because of economic difficulties in their homeland. In spite of poverty and hardships they worked diligently to establish their new Germantowns in the Saginaw Wilderness. It was because of these Saginaw German colonies that Michigan actively recruited additional Bavarian Germans. Until these colonies were established, no other group had successfully conquered the Saginaw Wilderness.

FOOTNOTES

1 *Teach My People the Truth*, pages 13 – 14

2 *Church Bells in the Forest*, pages 15 – 21

3 *Teach My People the Truth*, page 21

4 *Ibid,* pages 30 – 31

5 *Church Bells in the Forest,* pages 62 – 66

6 *Centennial Booklet on Frankentrost* & *Church Bells in the Forest,* pages 41 - 47

7 *Church Bells in the Forest,* pages 48 – 55 and *A Century of Grace,* Frankenlust

8 *A Century with Christ in Holy Cross,* pages 5-16

9 *Ibid,* pages 20 – 22

10 *A Century of Grace,* Amelith

11 *Church Bells in the Forest,* pages 56 – 61 and *One Hundred Years of Grace*

12 *Church Bells in the Forest,* pages 88 - 91

BIBLIOGRAPHY

A Century of Grace, St. Paul Evangelical Lutheran Church, Frankenlust, Michigan, 1848-1948

Centennial Booklet on Frankentrost, 1847-1947

Chapman, Chas. C., *History of Saginaw County Michigan,* Chicago, Illinois, 1881, pages 224-229, 263

Graebner, Theodore, *Church Bells in the Forest,* Concordia Publishing House, St. Louis, Missouri, 1944

Gremel, Edmund P., *A Century of Grace,* St. John's Amelith, 1852-1952

One Hundred Years of Grace, St. Michael's Evangelical Lutheran Church, Richville, Michigan, 1851-1951

Voss, Emil H. Pastor, *A Century with Christ in Holy Cross,* Saginaw, Michigan, 1849-1949

Zehnder, Herman, *Teach My People The Truth,* Story of Frankenmuth, Michigan, 1970

III In Pursuit Of The American Dream

America's great Western expansion began in the mid-1800's. The Northwest Territory had been divided into smaller regions. States had been organized and admitted to the Union. Thousands of restless settlers from the Eastern New England states abandoned their worn-out farms and began their trek to the new Western frontier. At the same time mass emigration was sweeping Northwestern Europe. Three distinct stages of world migration occurred during the nineteenth century.

The Celtic stage from the 1830's until 1860 brought immigrants from Ireland, Scotland, Wales, and Germany's Rhine Valley to America. In the Teutonic period from 1860 to 1890 most of the immigrants came from England, Scandinavia, Prussia, Saxony in Germany, and Bohemia in Austria. Over thirty-five million came to America during these two periods with half of them coming in the years 1847 through 1854. The second greatest number came in the decade from 1880 to 1890.

The Mediterranean or Slavic stage occurred from 1890 through 1914 during which seventeen million migrated to America. Immigrants from countries in Southeastern Europe—Poland, Hungary, Yugoslavia, and Italy—came during this era. Many were illiterate, unskilled menial laborers. The greatest number of immigrants came in the period from 1909 to 1914.[1]

This great Atlantic migration of people was one of the momentous world events which played a significant role in developing America's new frontier, including that of Michigan and Saginaw County. Over one million of these centuries-long stable people migrated to every continent in the world annually. Instead of interfering, their governments encouraged this grand exodus of people, viewing it as a solution to their country's economic problems. Emigration policies had not yet been adopted. When the immigrants came to America, they brought their European culture and traditions. A group of fellow immigrants would reproduce their homeland by forming a colony. These new immigrants could live in their colony in wilderness areas without interference by the established Americans. During this period of adjustment, they could perpetuate their European customs while gradually becoming assimilated into the new American culture. Ethnic societies, churches, and parochial schools in these colonies were instrumental in helping the foreign-born perpetuate their customs and traditions.[2]

During the Celtic and Teutonic periods Germans were the most desired immigrants. Their established German colonies in America proved that they were industrious, staunchly religious, family oriented, and educated. Protestant Europeans were also highly desired. Protestantism was considered individualistic while Catholicism was viewed as authoritarian. The church in Europe's feudal system dominated the individual's entire life. A peasant's life was one of supporting the landlord, the church and its cathedrals. Protestantism was a protest against this old feudal system, the authoritarian power and idealogy of the Roman Church. German Lutheran colonies had already been successfully established in Sebewaing and Ann Arbor, Michigan in the 1830's. By 1855, over five thousand German Lutherans lived in Ann Arbor. The German Lutheran colonies in Frankenmuth, Frankentrost, Frankenlust, and Frankenhilf provided excellent examples of an exemplary life in prompting the state to recruit additional German immigrants to Michigan.

The plight of both the Irish and Bavarian Germans was similar during this era. In the decade from 1820 to 1830, 50,724 Irish came to America. In the period from 1850 to 1860, 914,119 came to America. Then there was a steady decline from 1860 to 1937 with less than 100,000 coming annually in the later decades. When the potato crop failed in three successive years, Ireland's agricultural population was devastated and the plight of the people was indescribeable. Thousands of impoverished people left their homeland with nothing except the rags on their backs. Likewise, from 1846 to 1854, 900,000 Germans came to the United States. Half of these came in 1852 to 1854, with 215,009 coming in 1854. Another 100,000 came annually from 1866 to 1873. Another peak year occurred in 1882 with 250,630 arriving. After attaining a peak of 244,000 from 1891 to 1892, there was a steady decline in the ensuing years.[3]

A series of events resulting in mass emigration culminated over a period of years in Europe. The winter of 1829-1830 was one of the coldest in Europe. The lack of fuel affected Ireland and Bavaria the greatest. The winter of 1831-1832 resulted in crop shortages and escalating prices. Bread riots occurred. Granaries were raided and cattle slaughtered. Cholera caused additional devastation in both countries in 1832.

Violence erupted in Paris because of excessive food prices. This violence spread rapidly to Belgium, Germany, and Poland. German students formed secret societies to study constitutions, then held demonstrations to voice their radical theories. After thirty thousand people attended such a student demonstration at Hambach on May 27, 1832, peasants began rebelling and refused to pay taxes. Bavarian soldiers were stationed along the Rhine districts to preserve peace and order. These student radicals fled to Switzerland, France, England, then to America where they assumed positions of political and cultural leadership for the many German immigrants who followed in subsequent years. Dissension between the Old Lutherans of Prussia and Frederick William III worsened. These religiously oppressed people fled to America, settling in New York and Michigan. In the British Isles, the Elizabethan Poor Law of 1601 bound the laborer to his place of birth. In Ireland peasants sold their meager belongings and fled to America.

Since Napolean's defeat, Europe was experiencing the effects of thirty years of unbroken peace by the 1840's. There were no invading armies raiding the countryside, or bringing diseases and plagues, and no additional military taxes. Because husbands were at home instead of in foreign countries, families became larger and general overpopulation occurred throughout the country. Catholic priests encouraged early marriages, which resulted in large families whose children had little or no prospects for land or employment.[4]

With the steadily increasing agricultural population, acreage was divided into several small holdings no longer sustainable for several children to inherit. All tillable land had been utilized. The potato became the livelihood for millions. Every part of the potato was used. Besides supplying daily sustenance, the potato haulm was used to thatch cottages, and the peelings fed the family's livestock. A family survived on one and one-half acres. Crop overplanting yielded poor harvests. Grapes were grown on all available hilly land to supply Germany's wine industry. Agriculture in both Ireland and Bavaria was deteriorating. Poverty loomed everywhere. Pauperism flourished in city slums. The young and unemployed incited discontent in villages. Good harvests resulted in low prices. Famine followed poor harvests. Land values plummeted.

In a period of five years the weather patterns and disease caused yearly crop failures, wrecking havoc and devastation to millions. In 1842 when drought withered the pastures and cattle were slaughtered, the source of meat, milk and cheese was eliminated. The potato crop was small. Unusual wet weather hampered crops in 1843. In 1844 the wine crop was totally ruined. The potato fungus had first appeared in the Rhine Valley in 1829 and had steadily spread unchecked since that time. By 1845 crop failures along the Lower Rhine, in Scotland, England and Ireland were devastating the country. In 1846 crop failures had exhausted both Ireland and Germany. Poultry and livestock were slaughtered. The winter of 1846-1847 was one of extreme suffering with a shortage of fuel and food supplies. Northern and Eastern Germany were not experiencing crop failures but were also overpopulated.[5]

With each succeeding year of crop failures and famine, people were continually talking about emigration and America's critically short labor supply. Each spring thousands of peasants poured into Germany's port cities waiting days for transportation to America. Each new year brought a larger number of people than before preparing to emigrate. Three-quarter million German immigrants were peasants and artisans who were not concerned with the ongoing political revolution. Only a few thousand political refugees fled to America or other countries but often times returned to Germany. When an entire social class became impoverished, the centuries-long orderly society became chaotic. Emigration was the governments' solution to its overpopulation, economic problems, and famine. There were few legal formalities involved to emigrate. Restrictions were not instituted until new European events began culminating in the Crimean War later in the century. By then the mass exodus of people had resulted in more favorable economic conditions for those people still remaining in the homeland.

Several factors influenced Bavarian Germans to come to America. In 1824 Gottfried Duden migrated to America, settling on a Missouri farm. He returned to Germany in 1827, and in 1829 published a periodical with a series of letters describing his American experiences. He vividly described everyday life on a farm, spring planting, bountiful harvests, primeval forests, flowing rivers, glorious sunsets, moonlight nights, the absence of overbearing soldiers, clergymen, and tax collectors. He wanted a German-American city to be established in the West so that the centuries-old German culture and traditions could be transplanted to American soil and perpetuated for future generations. His writings were just the beginning of many events that inspired harassed peasants to emigrate to America.[6]

Romanticism permeated European fiction, poetry, and religion. American author James Fenimore Cooper's Leatherstocking Tales had been translated into several languages and sold around the world in the 1830's. Readers were thrilled with exciting adventures in the northern woods and western prairies. Germans became dissatisfied with their own monotonous, impoverished life. Village reading clubs were organized by local ministers who avoided political topics. Club members purchased books on history, travel and American literature, then shared them with other club members.[7]

Public education in both the British Isles and Germany helped to foster emigration. Children were taught several languages, including English, in Ireland. Children learned about new countries with abundant, rent-free land in their geography classes. Many Irish and Germans were first inspired to emigrate in their early childhood classrooms.

In the 1830's and 1840's emigration was carefully planned. Those planning to leave could read about their intended destination in gazetteers, geographies, newspapers, and shipping advertisements. Ever since the first colonial settlements in North America, it had become standard practice for several states, land companies, railroads, and shipping merchants to employ agents, both abroad and in American ports to encourage immigrants to come to America, then to selected states.

By the mid-1800's the Northwest Territory had been divided into states. Much labor was needed in developing the natural resources, building towns, roads, bridges, and canals. These new immigrants represented potential voters, laborers, farmers, taxpaying citizens, and investors to states, landowners, and shipping agents. Many newspaper ads, handbills, and personal appeals were made to immigrants, foreign consuls, and influential Europeans and Americans. Emigrant societies were organized in many German villages in the 1830's. By the 1850's emigration had become big business with several foreign agents in nearly every village.[8]

But the greatest influences of all were the letters written back home by those who had already emigrated to America. Because there was no organized mail delivery, it generally took six months or more for written correspondence to reach Germany. Even though letters told of many hardships on the American frontier, they spelled out the bountiful life in America. One day's wages in America were the equivalent of one acre of Germany's yearly harvest. The German could sell all his possessions, use the money for transportation to America, then work diligently and purchase an even larger farm than he could ever expect to own or inherit in Germany. After all, one's true Fatherland was not the country itself, but the habits, customs, family ties, friendship, and language of its citizens. These could all be established in new German-American colonies. German loyalty and patriotism could be re-established in their new adopted country.

The number of Europeans immigrating to America in the decade from 1830 to 1840 had increased five times that of the preceding decade. The emigrant had become an important article of commerce to the shippers. American tobacco and cotton had been regular exports to Europe since colonial days. In return Europe exported factory and workshop goods to America. Outward-bound cargoes from America carried heavier loads than the lighter return loads. In colonial times the return ships carried the African slave trade. Now the returning ships were crowded with impoverished immigrants seeking a new life in America.

Germans departed their homeland from three main ports. LeHavre, France was the largest port. LeHavre was enlarged to handle the teeming German immigrant tide. Steamboats and ships brought many immigrants on the Seine River to LeHavre docks. However, several Germans and Dutch began their trek from home in the same manner that pioneers began their new life in the American West. Long, winding

This Lutheran church has been standing in Germany since 1458. Some of the original settlers in Amelith had been members of this church as well as their ancestors who had been buried in this church yard for several generations. The German Lutheran churches built in the Saginaw missionary colonies resemble the churches in Germany.

Evang.-Luth. Pfarrkirche in Haundorf/Mfr.
1458/1958

horse and covered wagon trains traveled from the German-French border, camping along the way until reaching LeHavre. In LeHavre, there were always several thousand Germans lodged in all available inexpensive housing, awaiting departure which sometimes took up to six weeks. American ships brought Southern cotton to LeHavre, then returned crowded with immigrants to New Orleans, the major cotton port. Because the Southern climate did not appeal to the Germans, they paid $2.50 for Mississippi River passage to St. Louis and Cincinnati where large German-American cities were established.

Maryland and Virginia tobacco ships unloaded at Bremen to supply Germany, Austria, and Switzerland. By 1842 Bremen had become a major emigration port. Transportation barriers on the Rhine River's main tributaries were removed. Daily steamship service brought emigrants from the remote villages of Southern Germany and Holland up the Rhine River to Bremen. The Main River provided transportation from the states of Hesse and Bavaria; the Neckar River from Wurttenberg; and the Weser River from the states of Hanover and Westphalia. American ships leaving Bremen returned to Baltimore and New York with their crowded immigrant cargo.

The third port at Hamburg provided daily steamship service across the North Sea to Hull, England. From there the immigrants traveled on canals to Liverpool where they embarked for New York.[9]

Canadian timber merchants traveled to Ireland regularly. Primeval forests in Ireland had long ago disappeared. Canadian ships returned with Irish pork, eggs, and butter to the St. Lawrence region or Quebec. The Quebec route was least expensive, and thousands of Irish immigrants arrived at that port, then walked into America. They discovered that more land was available and there was a greater demand for unskilled labor in the United States. A shorter, less expensive journey from Ireland sailed to Halifax, St. John, and St. Andrews. From there the immigrants either sailed to other American ports or traveled through the wilderness to Maine.

In 1850 over two hundred thousand people left the United Kingdom for America, and four-fifths of them were Irish. Many had been saving for years to pay their transportation to America. Martin Doyle's *Hints on Emigration to Upper Canada* listed items for emigrants to take on their journey. Money was unsafe. The potato famine in 1846-1847 impoverished so many that mass migration followed. In 1851, some five thousand emigrants left weekly for America. By 1854 thousands took only the rags on their backs and very few, if any, personal possessions. Some parishes, local governments, and emigrant societies paid transportation fares for the most destitute.

Restrictions on Canadian ships were withdrawn. Some sailing vessels had cabins, but most immigrants traveled steerage in the cargo space. The overcrowded vessels carried from 450 to 517 passengers. The nine weeks at sea were extremely difficult. Passengers were confined between decks. There was always a shortage of food and water. The more fortunate brought enough of their own food of potatoes, flour, biscuits, butter, bacon, fish, spirits, molasses, and vinegar to last the entire trip. Keeping clean was impossible. Monotony, seasickness, and lack of privacy fostered discontent. Dancing was the usual pastime on shipboard. Frequent storms at sea hurled passengers from their berths, scattering people, food, and objects around the crowded steerage area. The overcrowded conditions often led to disease, death, and burial at sea. Epidemics of typhus fever, cholera, and measles often struck at sea. More than one million died in Ireland at the height of the potato famine.

But many more than this died at sea. At times nearly seventeen out of one hundred died on their journey to America. American ships leaving German ports were safer even though they were overcrowded. Overall conditions on American ships were better, but were still deplorable. Not as many Germans lost their lives at sea as did the Irish.[10]

Michigan's population was only 32,000 in 1830. With statehood in 1837 the population had increased to 175,000. Before 1835 only two million acres of land had been sold. In 1836, 4,189,823 acres were sold to settlers and speculators. Wildcat banks emerged overnight. Michigan Fever swept the country. Statehood brought optimism in spite of the Panic of 1837. Immigration stopped. Settlers from the East lacked the funds to move West. The state needed new labor to develop its natural resources and bring prosperity to Michigan. Legislators began looking to the German immigrants as homesteaders and a source of new labor. By the mid-1840's several German Lutheran peaceful farming, thriving colonies were already established in the Saginaw Valley. These future taxpayers would contribute to a stable law-abiding society.[11]

Although other states in the Northwest Territory were successfully employing emigrant agents, Michigan's Governor John A. Barry refused to create the position. In February, 1843 Dr. Louis Cavalli was hired by large landowners in Detroit to recruit in New York. He distributed handbills and directed eleven hundred immigrants to Michigan. In 1845 self-appointed agent Edmund B. Bostwick of Grand Rapids distributed handbills in New York. Several hundred German immigrants settled in the Grand River Valley.

In January, 1845 State Senator Edwin M. Cust of Livingston County introduced a petition for a Foreign Emigration Agency at New York. Governor Barry signed the law on March 24. On April 19 he appointed

Judge John Almy of Grand Rapids as the state's first official agent to live in New York. Only seven hundred dollars was allocated for expenses with another sixty dollars per month for compensation. Almy was already in New York representing large landowners in Kent, Ottawa, and Ionia Counties but he then began promoting the entire state. His six-page pamphlet, *State of Michigan, 1845—To Emigrants,* written in both English and German gave a map and general and statistical information of interest to immigrants. He published two editions of the pamphlet with five thousand copies being translated into several languages and distributed in Europe by foreign consuls and emigrant societies. He continued recruiting in New York until November 20, and then the post was abandoned. Through Almy's influence a Dutch colony from Holland under Reverend A .C. VanRaalte was established in western Michigan in November, 1846.

In 1847, Governor E. Ransom recognized the economic and social advantages that the many German and Dutch farming communities had already brought to Michigan. These hardy, industrious, frugal, religious communities would prove valuable assets to Michigan. After the Legislature passed the Emigration Agent Bill on February 1, 1849, the Governor appointed Senator and Prosecuting Attorney Edward H. Thomson of Flint in April. Thomson was born in 1810 in England, educated at Boston and came to Michigan in 1837. He specifically targeted Germans, Dutch, and Northern Irish if they were Protestant and not entirely destitute. Only seven hundred dollars was allocated for his New York living expenses until November, 1849.

Thomson published two editions of the forty-seven page *Emigrants Guide To The State Of Michigan* in both English and German. The first seven thousand copies were paid by the state; the second seven thousand copies were paid by Saginaw County. The pamphlet gave a map, a history of the state and information about rails, climate, markets,

An Emigranten.

New-York, den 1. Juni 1849.

Der Unterzeichnete ist von Sr. Excellenz, dem Gouverneur des Staates Michigan zum Agenten dieses Staates ernannt worden. Seit 12 Jahren daselbst ansäßig, erlaubt er sich, den Einwanderern in Folgendem Thatsachen vorzulegen, welche dieselben vielleicht veranlassen möchten, bei der Wahl ihres künftigen Wohnortes diesem Staate vor andern den Vorzug zu geben.

Michigan gehört zu den westlichen Staaten der Union und besteht aus zwei Halbinseln. Die größere dieser Halbinseln wird nördlich von der Meerenge von Mackinaw, östlich von den Seen Huron, St. Clair und Erie, und den Flüssen St. Clair und Detroit, südlich von den Staaten Ohio und Indiana, und westlich vom See Michigan begränzt. Dieser Hauptheil des Staates umfaßt 288 Meilen in der Länge, 190 Meilen in der Breite, mit einem Flächeninhalt von 38,000 engl. Quadratmeilen oder 24,320,000 Ackern. Die Zahl der Bevölkerung belief sich im Jahre 1810 auf 4528, im Jahre 1820 auf 9048, im Jahre 1830 auf 31,639, im Jahre 1840 auf 212,269, im Jahre 1845 auf 304,273, während man dieselbe jetzt auf circa 400,000 anschlägt.

Im Jahre 1845 zählte man 31 organisirte Provinzen (Counties) mit folgender Bevölkerung:

Provinzen:	Bevölkerung:	Provinzen:	Bevölkerung:
Allegan	3,185	Lapeer	5,314
Barry	2,672	Lenawee	23,011
Berrien	7,941	Livingston	10,789
Branch	9,070	Mackinac	1,007
Calhoun	15,719	Macomb	13,519
Cass	8,078	Monroe	13,305
Chippewa	1,017	Oakland	30,254
Clinton	3,411	Ottawa	1,438
Eaton	4,613	Saginaw	1,214
Genesee	9,266	Shiawassee	2,339
Hillsdale	11,625	St. Clair	7,030
Ingham	5,267	St. Joseph	10,097
Ionia	5,014	Van Buren	3,743
Jackson	16,852	Washtenaw	26,979

Two pages from Thompson's Emigrants Guide To The State Of Michigan dated June 1, 1849 printed in both English and German is reproduced here. Eddy Collection

agriculture, and commerce.

As a successful recruiter, Thomson enlisted the assistance of several

TO WESTERN EMIGRANTS.

NEW YORK, June 1, 1849.

THE undersigned, having become the Agent for the State of Michigan, by appointment from his excellency Governor Ransom, and entered upon the discharge of his duties, with a view of inducing immigration into the State which he represents, and which has been his home for the past twelve years, offers to the emigrant the following statement of *facts*:—

MICHIGAN is one of the Western United States, and consists of two peninsulas, *the principal* of which is bounded north by the straits of Mackinaw, east by Lake Huron, St. Clair river, Lake St. Clair. Detroit river, and Lake Erie, south by the States of Ohio and Indiana, and west by Lake Michigan. This main portion of the State is 288 miles long, and at a medium 190 miles broad, containing 38,000 square miles, or 24,320,000 acres. In 1810, the population was 4,528; in 1820, 9,048; in 1830, 31,639; in 1840, 212,269; in 1845, 304,273: while the population at this time, by those well qualified to judge of the vast increase during the past four years, is estimated at not less than 400,000.

There were, in 1845, 31 organized counties, with the following population in each :—

Counties.	Population.	Counties.	Population.
Allegan	3,185	Lapeer	5,311
Barry	2,672	Lenawee	23,011
Berrien	7,911	Livingston	10,789
Branch	9,070	Mackinac	1,667
Calhoun	15,719	Macomb	13,519
Cass	8,078	Monroe	13,365
Chippewa	1,017	Oakland	30,288
Clinton	3,111	Ottawa	1,438
Eaton	4,613	Saginaw	1,218
Genesee	9,266	Shiawassee	3,829
Hillsdale	11,625	St. Clair	7,080
Ingham	5,267	St. Joseph	10,097
Ionia	5,011	Van Buren	3,743
Jackson	16,852	Washtenaw	26,979
Kalamazoo	10,122	Wayne	32,367

influential groups. The directors of New York's most powerful shippers and merchants, the Grinnell, Minturn & Co., already had its own agents in major European ports. Captain Elisha E. Morgan of its *Southhampton* distributed three thousand copies of Thomson's pamphlet in Europe. Morgan's route ran direct to London from the German ports in Bale, Frankfurt, Bavaria, Wurttenberg, Baden and Saxony. From these ports immigrants traveled to London, then crossed the Atlantic, reducing travel time from sixty days to twenty-seven days. Thomson also made arrangements with Norwegian, Dutch, and German consuls to have his pamphlet translated and distributed in their countries.

Charles L. Fleischmann was appointed U.S. Consul to Wurttemberg in June, 1849 and became Thomson's most important liason with Germany. Fleischmann published a pamphlet with a map of Michigan, giving favorable descriptions of Michigan, Saginaw and surrounding counties, and conditions that interested farmers. The pamphlet was widely circulated in Germany.

The ten-member Board of the New York Commissioners of Emigration, the mayors of New York City and Brooklyn, and presidents of New York's German and Irish Emigration Societies all helped Thomson in his recruitment efforts, endorsed his pamphlets, and aided the sick and indigent immigrants, protecting them from charlatans and swindlers. Publications from all these societies and Thomson were read every Sunday in the German churches. Upon arrival in New York, the immigrants were held twenty-four hours in quarantine at Castle Garden, and Thomson's pamphlet was also distributed there.

A total of twenty-eight hundred immigrants came to Michigan through Thomson's efforts. Although he urged the Governor to extend the Agent position, the Governor vetoed these bills twice. While in

New York, Thomson showed compassion for the immigrants, helping them to find lost relatives and caring for sick children. When he returned to Michigan in November, he continued helping German settlers in locating suitable land.[12]

In 1850, Herr Friedrich Koch and his daughter Caroline arrived in Frankenlust. After establishing Kochville Township, he planned to relocate his mining company at Amelith. When Koch returned to Germany, he published and sold *The German Colonies In The Neighborhood Of The Saginaw River,* giving a description of the Saginaw Valley and Amelith. This book influenced many Germans to come to the Saginaw Valley.

From 1851 to 1860, 748,740 Irish and 951,667 Germans came to America. By January, 1859 Governor Wisner noticed that the tide of immigration was passing by Michigan for other western states. Yet five-sixths of Michigan was still wilderness. A new bill authorizing an Emigrant Agent was passed February 15, 1859, allocating twenty-five hundred dollars for annual living expenses. The Governor appointed two Germans—Rudolph Diepenbeck of Detroit to live in New York and George F. Veenfliet of Saginaw to live in Detroit. Diepenbeck prepared a forty-seven page book of Michigan, explaining the Law of 1859 enabling settlers to obtain forty acres free for a homestead and giving descriptions of boundaries, population, climate, soil, natural resources, communication, educational systems, maps and guides for German immigrants to come to Michigan. In 1859, 27,070 Germans came to New York, but only 561, each with an average of ninety dollars in cash, came to Michigan. In 1860, 1086 Germans came to Michigan because of Diepenbeck's efforts. Diepenbeck advised the Governor that an Agent should be sent to Germany to recruit immigrants.

However, all further bills were defeated and no future recruitment efforts were made until April 3, 1869, when Governor Henry P. Baldwin signed a new bill. He appointed Max H. Allardt of East Saginaw as Commissioner of Emigration to live in Germany with a five thousand dollar expense account and John W. Reisig as Resident Agent to live in New York with a fifteen hundred dollar expense account. Allardt, born in 1829 in Prussia, came to the United States in 1832, lived in Cleveland and Detroit, then came to East Saginaw to practice law during the Civil War.

Allardt lived in Frankfort, Germany from August, 1869 until March, 1870 when he moved his office to Hamburg. He published an eight-page guide *Der Michigan Wegweiser* every six weeks. Altogether he published thirty different editions, the last being in 1875. Each guide updated information for potential emigrants. Allardt specifically stated that the German classes who would be successful in Michigan were *robust farmers, skillfull merchants, enduring miners, industrious laborers, enterprising capitalists.*

In October, 1869 he published the sixty-four page *Michigan, Its Advantages & Resources* with a complete map of Michigan. Over two thousand copies of the *Wegweiser* were circulated free in Germany, Bohemia, and Hungary. In 1870, twenty-five hundred Germans were destined for Michigan: five hundred fifty-seven came through Allardt's efforts. Reisig traveled to Germany in April and October, 1870 to assist emigrants and accompanied forty-six, then one hundred thirty-six on his return trips back to New York.

In 1872 Allardt published another one hundred twelve-page *Geographische Und Statistche Beschrei Bung Des States Michigan.* Even though 2,722 Germans came to Michigan because of his work, Governor

John J. Bagley thought the expenses were too great. He closed the New York office on November 1, 1873, and recalled Allardt from Germany in November, 1874. Allardt's largest single effort was the settling of Colony Saxonia in Sanilac County.

In 1876 six states abandoned their foreign agent positions. Settlers from Ohio, Indiana, New York, Pennsylvania, Germany, Scandinavia, and Holland were treking westward to settle in the wilderness areas. A new bill passed on June 10, 1881 allowed the Governor to appoint a Commissioner of Immigration at an annual salary of two thousand dollars. Frederick Morley of Detroit was appointed. His one hundred forty-four-page pamphlet *Michigan & Its Resources* was published in three editions: twelve thousand copies, then another twenty thousand, and then ten thousand. In 1881, five thousand copies were sent to Germany; in 1882, three thousand copies to Holland. In 1883, several copies were distributed in several states and Canada. No further contacts were made with foreign governments or in New York. Future immigrants would know about Michigan only from past publications still in circulation. Henry N. Walker of Detroit succeeded Morley as Commissioner. As editor of the *Detroit Free Press,* he undoubtedly publicized Michigan in newspapers.[13]

From New York, there were various routes settlers could take to reach Michigan. Some settlers drove their teams and covered wagons from Buffalo, New York across Ontario to Windsor, then crossed the Detroit River into Detroit. Another route followed along Lake Erie's southern side. Most immigrants came westward on the Erie Canal to Buffalo. Others drove their teams or walked along the Genesee Road across New York to Buffalo. From Buffalo almost all traveled by steamboat on Lake Erie to Detroit.

The Erie Canal was begun in 1817 stretching from Rome to Albany. Each year the canal was lengthened. It was completed in 1825, with a total of three hundred sixty miles from Buffalo on Lake Erie to Albany on the Hudson River. This all-water route from the Great Lakes to New York City played an instrumental role in helping settle and develop the natural resources in the Midwest. Instead of hauling freight over muddy roads, passengers and their freight now traveled the canal route. The great western trek of German immigrants utilized this route. The earlier immigrants had brought some freight. As immigration increased, people brought less freight and personal belongings.[14]

To reach Michigan most immigrants boarded a steamer at New York City and traveled northward up the Hudson River to Albany. From Albany to Buffalo, travel fare on a canal boat generally was $1.50. A trip lasted from seven to ten days. Rail travel between the two cities took thirty-six hours, but fare was $5.00 for an immigrant car or $9.75 for a seat in a passenger coach. From Buffalo to Detroit, immigrants traveled on lake vessels the entire length of Lake Erie. Steerage was $1.50 to $2.50, or a cabin cost $4.00 to $5.00. The boats sailed daily and the trip took twenty-four hours. On all types of transportation the immigrant carried his own food supply for the entire journey.

Reaching the Saginaw Wilderness was accomplished by land or water. From Detroit lumber steamers traveled through Lake St. Clair, Lake Huron, the Saginaw Bay to the mouth of the Saginaw River at Lower Saginaw (Bay City). Because there were no roads, steamers or tug boats provided river transportation to Saginaw City, a village of about three hundred inhabitants.

Traveling by land, some immigrants rode in farm wagons and walked from Detroit to Saginaw, or travelers could board the railroad from Detroit to Pontiac. This train engine pulled only one car about the size of a streetcar. When the car jumped the strap rails about every half

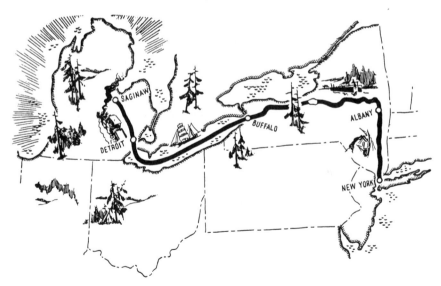

This map shows the method of travel and route that the Bavarian German colonists took from New York to Saginaw.

mile, passengers got off to help put the train back on the tracks. The train stopped often for its passengers to pick ripe blackberries along the route. The train traveled twenty-six miles in four hours. The trek from Pontiac to Saginaw took another two days. When a train track was built from Pontiac to Flint, travel time was shortened. Roads from Pontiac to Flint to Saginaw were practically nonexistent. The trip to the Saginaw Wilderness was through primeval forest, following Indian trails through the dark, silent, unbroken forest. It generally took about a week to travel by land from Detroit to Saginaw.

The immigrant who had traveled thousands of miles and endured all types of hardships now saw the publicized Saginaw Wilderness unfold before him. New challenges and different hardships awaited him. In every direction as far as the eye could see, stretched the dense, dark mysterious forest just waiting to be explored. Scattered here and there along the river bank were small clearings and log shanties inhabited by the lone settlers. Curtis Emerson's sawmill, boarding house, and Halls of Montezumas were the first signs of civilization viewed by those arriving on the River. This was the village of Saginaw City. By land, a traveler broke his way through dense forest and brush, following the Indian trails, and emerged around the Green Point clearing.

As East Saginaw and Saginaw City developed with the lumber industry, transportation improved and access to the Saginaws became much easier. With more lumber steamers plying the Great Lakes to New York, transportation to Michigan and the Saginaws became faster for later immigrants. The Saginaws soon became a bustling lumber port. Speculators, traders, investors, and settlers arrived on every returning lumber sailing vessel.

Michigan's population increased by leaps and bounds, due largely to

Europe's mass exodus of people. Michigan's population had increased to 749,113 in 1860. Its foreign born at that time consisted of 38,000 Germans, 36,000 Canadians, 30,000 Irish, 25,000 English and 5,000 Scots. By 1880, Michigan's population reached 1,636,331. In 1890, population was 2,093,889. Its foreign born numbered: 181,000 Canadians, 135,000 Germans, 55,000 English, 39,000 Irish, and 12,000 Scots.[15]

The large number of immigrants from the Celtic and Teutonic periods of European immigration had settled in the great American Midwest. They had established towns in the wilderness areas and they and their descendants were now concentrating on building those towns into prosperous industrial cities. Two lumber towns had also been established in the Saginaw Wilderness by these new immigrants and Eastern investors and were destined to become one of Michigan's most important prosperous, agricultural, and industrial cities.

FOOTNOTES

1   *The Atlantic Migration*, pages 9 – 11

2   *Ibid*, page 12

3   *One America*, page 104

4   *The Atlantic Migration*, pages 123 – 128

5   *Ibid*, page 220

6   *Ibid*, page 123

7   *Ibid*, pages 147 – 148

8   *Michigan Emigrant Agent*, page 3

9   *The Atlantic Migration*, Pages 185 – 199

10   *The Great Migration*, pages 34 – 44

11   *Michigan in Four Centuries*, pages 154 – 156

12   *Michigan Emigrant Agent*, pages 3 – 38

13   *Michigan Immigration*, pages 67 – 100

14   *Michigan Yesterday and Today*, pages 179 - 187

15   *Michigan in Four Centuries*, pages 293 - 295

BIBLIOGRAPHY

Bald, F. Clever, *Michigan in Four Centuries*, Harper & Brothers, Publishers, New York, 1954, pages 154 – 156, 262, 293 – 295

Bowers, David F., *Foreign Influences in American Life*, Peter Smith, New York, 1952

Brown, Francis J. & Roucek, Joseph Slabey, *One America*, Prentice-Hall, Inc., New York, 1937, 1945

Guillet, Edwin C., *The Great Migration, The Atlantic Crossing by Sailing Ship Since 1770*, Thomas Nelson & Sons, Toronto, London, New York, 1937

Hansen, Marcus Lee, *The Atlantic Migration 1607 –1860*, Harvard University Press, 1940

Lewis, Ferris E., *Michigan Yesterday and Today*, Hillsdale Educational Publishers, Inc., 1956, pages 157 – 163, 179 – 191, 258 – 261

Michigan History:
Michigan Immigration, XXVIII, 1944 by William L. Jenks, pages 67 – 100

Michigan Emigrant Agent: Edward H. Thomson, Volume 59, spring – summer, 1975, number 1-2 by Daniel E. Sutherland, pages 3 – 38

Rubenstein, Bruce A. and Ziewacz, Lawrence E., *Michigan, A History of the Great Lakes State*, Forum Press, 1981, pages 119 – 128

Saginaw Daily Courier, May 16, 1870, page 1; June 3, 1870, page 1; August 17, 1870, page 2

Part II
Natural Resources

The Saginaw Valley was rich in natural resources. Discovery of each new resource brought a new group of people into the Valley. Some of these people were transient, leaving as soon as the resource was exhausted. Others became permanent residents. Thousands of their descendants continue to live in the Saginaw Valley today.

Guess where on the Tittabawassa, Freeland, Mich.

Girls in long dresses paddle their canoes down the Tittabawassee River on a lazy Sunday afternoon as depicted in this postcard mailed in Saginaw in 1910. The lumber industry was long ago defunct, and the river was now used for recreational purposes.

IV Spring
on the Tittabawassee

The mighty Tittabawassee River had become a recreational river by the turn of the century. It was the perfect serene place for fishing, swimming, and boating on a Sunday afternoon. But this mighty river presented an altogether different scene during the preceding fifty years. It was one of Michigan's major rivers, fostering the lumber industry and bringing billions of logs to the many Saginaw River sawmills. The Tittabawassee River was instrumental in building the important Saginaw lumber town.

Michigan became the twenty-sixth state on January 26, 1837. Its entire population increased to 175,000. Almost the entire state was covered with primeval forest—a mature, virgin three-hundred-year-old forest untouched by man. Michigan was part of the immense Northern forest belt extending from Maine through New York and Pennsylvania to Minnesota, then up to Ontario and Quebec. Michigan's best pine both in quality and quantity came from the central portion of the Lower Peninsula.[1]

This vast, mysterious Michigan forest was a source of new wealth and adventure just waiting to be discovered. When Saginaw lumber was discovered in 1847, Eastern investors came in droves to purchase timber tracts in central Michigan. In the next forty-some years Michigan's green gold outproduced California's yellow gold by more than a billion dollars. Originally, the lumbermen were interested only in the white pine which grew in clumps on uplands and ridges with trees towering up to one hundred seventy feet high and having trunks up to five feet wide. These mature trees over forty years old were light weight and easily flotable.

First, an experienced timber cruiser would come to an area and survey the forest with binoculars to locate good stands of pines in tracts ranging from forty acres to eighty acres and having easy accessibility to rivers and streams. Eastern investors would then purchase the selected tracts from the United States Government for $1.25 per acre. David Ward was an experienced, important mid-Michigan cruiser who selected rich stands of timber in St. Clair County for Charles Merrill, a Maine lumberman, and for many Eastern investors who became wealthy lumber barons.[2]

The next step was to establish a lumber camp on the selected tract early in the fall. A lumber owner or operator might operate a dozen separate camps on his many timber tracts. Each camp was established for sixty to one hundred men. A gang of swampers and wood butchers would go into the forest in early fall to cut down trees, break a tote road, then build a camp. Several log shanties constructed with rough lumber covered with tar paper were built for a cook's camp, mess camp, men's camp, office, store, barn, and blacksmith shop. The men's camp had double-decker bunks of springy poles covered with cedar boughs. Each man's pillow was his *turkey*—his cloth grain sack in which he carried his spare clothing, a blanket, and personal items from home. The swampers cut a skidroad accessible from all points in the wooded tract and leading to the stream or river. A dump or rollway on the river bank was started by laying logs across skids. With the first good freeze, road

One of the rough buildings in a central Michigan lumber camp is shown. Whole, small logs are used for the roof. Teams of oxen and horses are shown with shanty boys. Slasinski Collection

sprinkling began. Each night the roadway was sprinkled with water from the stream until the road was solid paved with ice.

As soon as a camp was established, boats and trains would begin bringing supplies to the camp. With each trip a carload of woodsmen or shanty boys would also arrive. The men often walked some distance into the woods to find the logging camp. Each of these shanty boys was assigned to a job in which he was skilled—faller, chopper, sawyer, teamster, skidder, decker, loader, scaler, cook, blacksmith, etc. The logging industry was a highly skilled, organized operation.

Actual logging began with the arrival of freezing, snowy weather about mid-November. Two fallers worked in pairs, felling trees with a two-handled crosscut saw. When the tree was about to fall, one faller would yell out **TIMB-E-R-R-R!** As it echoed through the woods, all

Several tons of logs were loaded on sleighs and then pulled over icy roads by one team of horses to the river banking grounds. Slasinski Collection

shanty boys would move away from the falling tree. **TIMB-E-R-R-R!** **TIMB-E-R-R-R!** and crashing trees could be heard repeatedly all day long from all directions in the forest tract. Choppers followed the fallers trimming boughs from the fallen tree. Then sawyers came to saw the great trunk into manageable sawlogs. The average log was sixteen inches in diameter and was cut into sixteen foot lengths to equal one hundred forty-four board feet. Teamsters hooked skidding tongs to the cut logs and dragged them on travois down the skidroad to a decking platform. Logs were cross piled on several decking platforms along the skidroad. They became way stations for loading bobsleighs.

There was always a steady supply of logs coming to the skidroad from several destinations. Loaders and deckers helped teamsters load the sleighs to haul the logs to the river banking grounds. There the scalers and stampers recorded the board feet per log and stamped each log with a stamping iron to designate company ownership.

The shanty boys worked all winter from November through March in all kinds of weather, six days per week from dawn to dusk. The forest gradually receded leaving broad areas of tree stumps and brush. Cut-off logs stamped with the owner's log mark accumulated in mammoth piles on mid-Michigan's many streams and river banks. All logs were scaled and marked ready to float with the first spring thaw. Millions of logs accumulated in storage deposits and were frozen into snow and ice all along the logging streams.[3]

In the early years of Michigan's lumber industry streams and rivers were the main arteries of log transportation to the mills. Just prior to a spring river drive, a crew of men cleaned and deepened channels in the streams, by freeing them of rocks and trees to prevent log jams. Dams were constructed to control the flood stages so logs could be brought to mills in all months from April through November. During these months river hogs or drivers kept logs moving down rivers, broke up and prevented log jams, and retrieved stray logs. The men often became soaked in the water, slept and ate in the open. When the rivers had risen high enough for flotage prior to flood stage, the river rollway was broken open and logs were sent downstream on their journey to the mills.

Drivers wearing spiked boots and carrying peaveys rode the logs as they traveled down the waterway. Each driver had a sixteen inch square oilcloth sack in which he carried a blanket, dynamite, and his lunch of biscuits, cookies, doughnuts, ham, and eggs slung over his shoulder and tied down. Two wanigans or house boats floated down the river just behind the log drive. A cook's kitchen occupied one wanigan, and the other sleeping shack carried supplies. The cook placed the food in kettles on an outdoor table. Men filled their tin plates, then sat on the river bank to eat. Meals were sent ahead to the river drivers who slept and ate whenever and wherever they could. Drivers slept out in the open or in tents during the night.

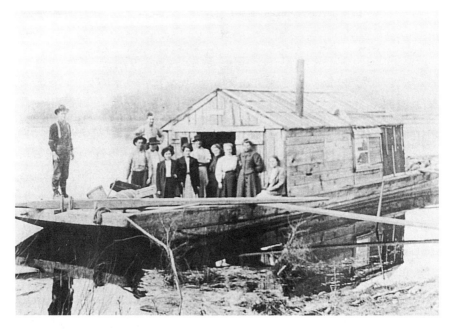

Generally two wanigans such as this one followed the river log drive. One wanigan carried supplies and the other served as the kitchen. Slasinski Collection

Drivers worked up to sixteen hours a day in all kinds of weather. Men jumped into water or floating ice hip high to roll stray logs back into the water to continue their journey. Drivers never changed their wet clothes; they dried on them. Everyone worked their utmost to get logs to their destination so that they would not be hung up until the following spring. Sackers brought up the rear of the log drive. They followed the river drivers and prodded the stray logs snarled on the river bank back into the river. When logs piled, rolled, and jammed in bends, it took several river hogs to control and direct them down stream. Several logging camp shanty boys were hired for the river drives and worked throughout the summer. When logging eventually became a year-round industry, river hogs became very skilled and worked all year driving logs.

The river drive was finished when the logs reached the booming grounds at the river's mouth. Rows of piles held the boomsticks which were long flat timbers chained end to end. At this point the river hogs' jobs ended and employees of a booming company took over.[4]

A large boom led to many smaller pocket booms which were built for each individual lumber owner. Pike poles were used to handle logs, sorting the log marks, rafting logs, and delivering them to sawmills. Logs were sorted by log marks into their individual booms. The head gap sorter carried a notebook with the marks, knew all the marks, and would pole logs into their respective booms. Logs in their pocket booms were then arranged side by side to form a raft. Pin whackers who were youngsters or light-weight men threw rope over the logs and drove a wooden V-pin into each log over the rope to secure the raft. Rafts were moved into the navigation channel to be towed by tug boats to Saginaw River sawmills. During lumber's heyday, the Saginaw River was

The Tittabawassee Boom Co. has sorted logs by log marks into individual booms for the different mill owners. The men walked on the logs to sort and cross the river.

The men from the Tittabawassee Boom Co. are lining up logs and building rafts which will be towed down the river to the Saginaw River and the mill owner's sawmill. Photos from Slasinski Collection

continuously full of logs. However, state law required that one-half of a river channel must be kept free for boat transportation. Therefore, only one-half of a river could be used by booming companies for their log rafts.

From lumber's beginning, state laws were continually being enacted to regulate the industry. An 1842 Act required log marks to be registered in the county where the logs would be manufactured into lumber. By 1859 laws required owners to mark the ends of their logs in a distinctive manner and register their marks. There were also laws dealing with log thievery. An 1855 Act permitted booming companies to run, drive, boom, raft logs, timber, and lumber and regulate the flotage. In 1864 booming companies could incorporate and enforce log mark registration

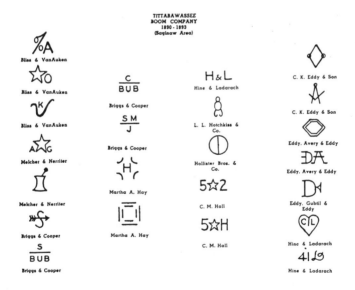

These are just some of the many log marks which identified the mill owners for whom the Tittabawassee Boom Co. sorted logs. Logs were already marked at the lumber camp before they began their spring drive down the rivers.

requirements.[5]

The Cass, Flint, Shiawassee, Bad, and Beaver Rivers each had separate booming companies to drive logs, sort, and raft logs to be brought to the Saginaw River mills. Charles Merrill was already a wealthy lumberman when he founded the Charles Merrill & Co. for booming in 1856. His Merrill Boom was located where the Merrill Bridge (present-day Center Road) crossed the Tittabawassee River. During the company's existence until 1864, it boomed out 1,700,000,000 feet of logs. Its sorting boom was one long boom with smaller booms along its end, but it was not efficient for the large volume of logs yet to come on the Tittabawassee.

The Articles of Corporation for the Tittabawassee Boom Co. were signed on February 4, 1864, allowing the corporation to operate for thirty years. The company would boom and raft logs on the Saginaw, Tittabawassee, Chippewa, and Pine Rivers. Capital was $50,000, but only $25,000 was actually paid by stockholders. Capital stock was divided into five hundred shares with twenty-five stockholders, all of whom had logs boomed through Charles Merrill & Co. Shares ranged from five to forty shares each with Joseph A. Whittier and Thomas Merrill being the largest stockholders each with forty shares. Temple E. Dorr was elected president and Joseph A. Whittier was secretary.[6]

The Boom Company would raft and deliver logs to owners at any point before the head of the Merrill Boom. The company would receive the logs in their booms on the Pine, Chippewa, and Tittabawassee Rivers near Midland. The price of booming was established as follows:

Logs 30' or less   50 cents per M (thousand board feet measure)

Logs 30' – 50'   70 cents per M

Logs 50' & more $1.00 per M

Rafting logs & rope   10 cents to 30 cents per M

If the log owner didn't take the rafted logs into its company's boom and return   the raft rope within a reasonable time, the owner was additionally liable for the wages and expenses of the men who worked on the raft.

The Boom Company built and maintained boarding houses throughout its decades of operation. In January 1866, boarding houses were built at the Green Point Boom for forty-eight men, State Road Bridge Boom for twelve men, Merrill Boom for forty-five men, and Fitzhugh Boom in Midland for forty-five men. Ice and pin houses were also built at each of the four locations. The boarding houses were gradually expanded so that by 1874 there were nine total. A yearly maintenance expense was to replace ice or pin houses at one of the boarding house locations.

The company invested capital regularly in building dams to control the flood waters and keep the logs being driven onto the Tittabawassee throughout the summer. Samual Sias was hired to build its dams. In May 1866, the company spent $1,000 to build a dam on the Salt River. In September a dam was built on the Chippewa River. In December 1868, a dam was built on the Tittabawassee River above Midland at a cost of $3,000. These three dams adequately controlled flooding to move logs whenever desired. The low water stage throughout the summer of 1874 necessitated construction of another new dam below Sixteen at a cost of $4710.15. Without this dam it was impossible to have moved logs from the rear of the Tittabawassee.

Bridge building was another regular expense incurred by the company. In June 1868, the bridge across the Chippewa River had been swept away by high water, ice, and logs. The town of Homer and Midland

County paid $1700 and the Boom Company paid $300 towards rebuilding the bridge. In December 1869, the Boom Company had to clear its logs from the Tittabawassee River and aid in building the bridge at Freeland. In November 1874, the new State Road Bridge (present-day M-46) was built with the company's assistance.

The Boom Company continually leased, purchased, built, and maintained its many miles of river booms. In 1866, the company already maintained fourteen miles of river booms and eight miles of shore booms valued at $127,987.49, but it also purchased the Fitzhugh River Booms in Midland for $3,000 and signed a ten year lease for use of the river front. Booms were built on land rented from James Fraser above Wiltsie Ferry, and on land owned by Mr. Shields and Mrs. Chamberlain. John and Peter McGregor were paid twenty-five cents per rod for leasing their river front for twelve years beginning in January 1867. The Green Point Boom grounds and land for a boarding house were leased from W.L.P. Little for $2,000 yearly for ten years. In 1869, a storage boom was built below Zilwaukee to store logs which were then delivered to Bay City. Whenever heavy ice damaged booms, boomage prices also increased.

Log jams were continuous problems for booming companies. The 1869 drive season resulted in one hundred ten miles of logs laying in a solid jam in the Tittabawassee River and its tributaries. This was the equivalent of 348 million feet of 1,277,241 logs scaling 277,026,057 board feet. In June the river below Midland was so filled with logs that they were crowded out of the channel and flooded the river flats along the river all summer long. The company paid $6,000 for damages to landowners. By January 1870, all these logs except for sixty million feet had been rafted out.

The river drive in 1873 brought a one-hundred-thirty-mile solid log jam from six miles above Edenville, six miles above the boom on the mouth of the Little Cedar, and on the Tobacco River. The river was filled to utmost capacity down to the State Road Bridge Boom. The Pine was solid from its mouth to Bailey's Farm five miles below St. Louis and five miles above boom limits. The Chippewa was full five miles along the road. There were six hundred million feet of logs in the Sturgeon, Big Salt, Chippewa, Salt and smaller streams. The streams were filled two to five logs deep and were flooded onto the river flats and farms, washing away portions of the bank and flooding entire farms with logs. Many logs laid on farms until they were put back into the river. Dredging was done at several booms, and three hundred thirty-eight new piles were driven to enlarge rafting capacity and widen the

This famous Goodridge Bros. photo of the Tittabawassee River was taken where the present-day Imerman Park winds down to the river. The 130 mile log jam in 1873 had logs piled two to five deep on all logging streams down to the State Road Bridge Boom (present-day Gratiot Road.) Slasinski Collection

transportation channels.

The company paid annual crop damages and rental fees to land owners along the rivers. On July 1, 1867, William Kelly was paid two hundred dollars for damages to his farm on Pine River, and his land was leased for thirty dollars per year until 1879. On June 28, 1869, S. Bailey of Midland was paid three hundred dollars for damages to ten acres of meadowland and stagnant water on another three acres of land. Eli R. Bailey was paid three hundred dollars; Margaret Hall of Freeland fifty dollars for her garden and meadowland. Nelson Munger was paid five hundred dollars for seventeen acres of corn and twelve acres of grassland which were flooded four times—three times by logs and once by normal flood waters. On January 7, 1876, Mrs. J.F. Paine and James Frazer presented their bills for damages. Thomas Parker was paid twenty dollars per year for using his shore line from 1875 through 1877.

Stealing logs was a constant problem. In 1868, a sawmill near Freeland was sawing off log marks, then manufacturing the logs into shingles. The Boom Company took action to repossess their stolen logs. Stealing logs about Midland and along the Saginaw River had become a regular annoyance by 1879. In fact, log stealing had become so rampant in Michigan that a law was enacted in 1879 to provide penalties for unlawfully changing marks and to make manufacturers liable for processing stolen property. Log owners were given the right to search booms for their property. Outsmarting the other fellow became an acceptable rule of the day.

Buying rope and rafting pins were yearly necessary big expense items. In January 1866, the company paid $14,753.13 for rope and $3800 for rafting pins. Rope prices averaged twenty-three cents per pound. The company needed ten tons of rope and three to four casks of chain to begin the season. In 1867 the company spent $10,260.08 on rope. Rope used the second year was not dependable in strong currents, and it was entirely useless by the third year. In November 1869, the company negotiated with Mr. Raymond to use his Patent Crotch Rafting Pin. Raymond sold the pin manufacturing machine for $3,000. From 1874 through 1880 the Boom Company contracted with D. Hardin & Co. to make and deliver crotch pins at $3 per M.

Often booming companies would subcontract rafting to an agent. In May 1873, Brewer, Carrington & Co. occupied the second story of the company's office at 632 N. Water Street. This agent hired its own men and boats, gathered all stray logs on the Saginaw River and delivered them in rafts to mill operators. In 1875 Brewer gathered and delivered ten thousand logs from the Saginaw River and towed another ten thousand logs to the holding booms. Brewer was paid $6200 for his rafting and rope. By January 1876, the old logs in the Saginaw River contained eleven hundred different log marks. These had accumulated over four years so some marks were obliterated from exposure. Agent Avery & Co. retrieved and delivered them to their proper owners.

Wages for the men varied yearly. Wages in 1866 were less than the prior year and were set at twenty-eight dollars or less per month. In January 1868, Superintendent Bell was paid twenty-five dollars for using his horse and buggy for company business. Labor and board were the company's greatest expenses. In 1868 labor and board totalled $74,423.25. In 1872 wages were set at four dollars per week for the man boarding himself. Incentives were used to recruit and keep reliable workers. In March 1873, every man making the greatest number of rafts would receive an extra six dollars per month. Those having the second greatest number of rafts would get four dollars extra per month.

Men had to work at least twenty days before being paid. This practice eliminated some job turnover by discouraging men from leaving for easier or safer work. The agent in charge of the company's business would receive fifteen hundred dollars per year. In September 1873, the men's wages were reduced twelve and one-half per cent. Agent Kimball was paid two thousand dollars per year. Labor costs totalled $92,531.08 for 1874.

Booming prices also fluctuated from year to year. In 1875 prices for booming and delivery would be five cents per M less than that in 1874. By 1877 booming and delivery was twenty-six cents per M. In 1878 booming increased to thirty cents per M.

The company's profits and losses fluctuated from year to year. On January 8, 1866, the first total stock dividend of $25,000 was paid to investors since their initial investment in 1863. Another $40,000 dividend was paid in 1867; $45,000 in 1868; $30,000 in 1869; $25,000 in 1870. Thereafter, $20,000 was paid yearly from 1874 through 1877. The dividend decreased to $15,000 per year thereafter.

President Joseph Shaw and Secretary Joseph A. Whittier were each paid five hundred dollars and each member on a Board of Directors committee received one hundred dollars in 1866. 1866 was one of the best years in booming. By 1880, the president's salary was fixed at $5,000.[7]

Throughout its thirty years of operation, the Tittabawassee Boom Company became a giant in the booming industry, booming and rafting more board feet than any other Michigan booming company. By the company's conclusion in 1894, it had rafted a total of 11,848,549,293 board feet.[8] Each year had seen an increase in the number of logs boomed. In 1868 the company boomed 985,923 logs. A high year was 1874 with 1,979,813 boomed. But in 1877, the total boomed was 2,352,441 logs.

After the Tittabawassee Boom Co. ceased operations in 1894, a new Tittabawassee River Boom Co. operated at its office at 632 N. Water from 1894 through 1896. The Tittabawassee Boom & Raft Co. replaced this company in 1897.

In the industry's early years the weather controlled the timber harvested in Michigan forests and served as a natural check and balance on supply and demand. Unfavorable seasons limited overproduction and helped in keeping the market stable. In the 1868 – 1869 season harvesting began late because the snow was late and sparse. In January Burt's Camp on the Tittabawassee River removed the sleighs, and teams hauled logs on the bare ground. The camp could only harvest one tenth of what it should have done that winter.[9]

However, by 1880 the Michigan forests were drastically depleted and weather conditions no longer prevailed in getting the logs to mills since the log railroad, pole and tram roads were used instead. Although the cost of logging had increased one dollar per M, processed lumber was commanding higher prices. Lumber on mill docks was already sold before being processed since advance contracts were being negotiated.

The Saginaw mills' supply source had declined to only the Tittabawassee and its tributaries and the Rifle and AuGres Rivers. The Flint and Shiawassee Rivers were already depleted in 1879 and were only able to furnish about two million feet, part of which was hard timber. The Bad River was steadily declining and could only supply twelve million feet which would be manufactured at St. Charles mills. Although eighty million feet would be produced on the Rifle River, only seventy million feet would reach Saginaw. On the AuGres, only eighty per cent of its ninety million feet would reach Saginaw. Other Saginaw sources were: Kawkawlin eight million feet, Shore Pine fifteen million feet, and AuSable eighteen million feet. Railroads would bring another ninety million feet to Saginaw mills. Flint & Pere Marquette Railroad would bring seventy million and Michigan Central would bring twenty million. Summer logging was necessary to make up quota deficiencies.[10]

In 1868 it was already thought that lumber had reached its zenith and would only last another fifteen years. But in 1888 the Michigan timber supply still exceeded the amount harvested. The logging railroad was penetrating the territory previously inaccessible to the logging streams. *The Beginning of the End* was in sight. The Upper Peninsula and Georgian Bay Country in Canada were being tapped by the lumbermen. As long as a Canadian export duty was not imposed, Canada would be a channel for years of future prosperity. Throughout the summer of 1888 immense rafts, some containing five million feet, were towed from the Upper Peninsula successfully to the mouth of the Saginaw River. [11]

On August 17, 1887, the largest raft ever—eight million feet—was towed by three powerful tugs—*Mocking Bird, Gladiator,* and *International.* It was valued at $100,000 and when sawed, it would aggregate $200,000. The raft reached Bay City from AuTrain and Lake Superior. It was brought in a big boom and blocked the entire river channel. Tugs moved it in sections down the Saginaw River.[12]

In 1890 towing logs by rafts to the Saginaw River had become an essential part of the lumber business. Immense rafts were brought down from Green Bay, Georgian Bay region, Lake Superior and Straits of Mackinac. Large lake tugs—*Sea Gull, Mocking Bird, Music, Waldo Avery,*

Niagara, Justice Fields, Peter Smith—owned by Reid Towing & Wrecking Co. and Captain Ben Boutell of Bay City brought four to eight million feet of logs at a time and seldom lost a log. Even when a raft was broken apart in a storm, it was easily retrieved. Tug owners paid lumbermen for every log not delivered.[13]

Log transportation by logging streams continued on a drastically reduced scale through most of the 1890's. Upper Peninsula and Canadian timber kept the lumber industry going into the early 1890's. However, when Canada placed an embargo on its timber, the Saginaw River sawmills' supply dwindled drastically and its supply remained only from the Upper Peninsula. However, by the late 1890's both the Michigan and the Saginaw lumber industry had become exhausted.

FOOTNOTES

1 *Michigan's White Pine Era*, page 10

2 *Ibid*, pages 13 – 15

3 *Michigan Log Marks*, pages 15 – 19

4 *Ibid*, pages 19 – 28

5 *Ibid*, page 12

6 *Tittabawassee Boom Co. Notes*, Volume I

7 *Ibid*, Volumes I & II

8 *Michigan Log Marks*, page 39

9 *Saginaw Daily Enterprise*, 1/13/1869

10 *Saginaw Daily Courier*, 4/17/1880

11 *Saginaw Evening News*, 7/31/1888

12 *Saginaw Evening News*, 8/12 & 8/17/1887

13 *Saginaw Evening News*, 1/7/1890

BIBLIOGRAPHY

Maybee, Rolland H. *Michigan's White Pine Era*, Bureau of History, Michigan Department of State, 1988

Michigan Log Marks compiled by Work Projects Administration, Published by Michigan Agricultural Experiment Station, 11/1941, 1/1942

Mills, James, *History of Saginaw County*, 1918, Volume I, pages 393 – 425, Volume II, pages 1-4, 17-18

Saginaw County Historian, *Sawmills of Saginaw County*, Volume I, Issue l, Bastian Bros. & Co., 1983

Saginaw Daily Courier, 4/17/1880, page 2, c. 2

Saginaw Daily Enterprise,
1/13/1869, page 1, c. 4;
1/15/1869, page 1, c.3;
12/29/1869, page 1, c.2

Saginaw Evening News,
8/12/1887, page 7;
 8/17/1887;
 7/31/1888, page 4;
 1/7/1890, page 6, c.2;
 5/1/1890, page 3

Tittabawassee Boom Co. Minutes,
Volume I – 2/1864 – 1/1873
Volume II-2/1873 – 12/1880

V SAGINAW
RIVER SAWMILLS

Harvey Williams was building engines for Great Lakes steamboats in Detroit when he decided to build the first steam mill in the Saginaw Valley in 1834. He manufactured the machinery similar to that used on the steamer *Superior*. With great difficulty he transported the machinery over rivers and through primeval forests to Saginaw on sleighs. His cousins, Gardner D. and Ephraim S. Williams, soon joined him in this first steam mill venture near Mackinaw Street on the Saginaw River in Saginaw City. Millwright Joel L. Day of Bay City installed the first muley saw ever used in the Valley. There was a single run of stone for grinding cracked corn. The first lumber cut in this mill was used for the early settlers' building needs. The mill cut about two thousand feet of planks in twelve hours. Logs were brought in from the streams on the Tittabawassee River. The 1835 – 1836 season provided a profitable business for the mill owners.[1]

Norman Little commissioned Harvey Williams to build another muley sawmill, dwelling, boarding house, barn, and blacksmith shop in East Saginaw on the present-day City Hall site for the Mackie, Oakley & Jenninson Co. of New York in 1836. This 55' x 120' building had three upright saws, one butting saw, one edging table, and a seventy-five horsepower engine with three boilers. The mill had the capacity to cut three million feet of lumber. The mill was closed in 1844.

The Panic of 1837 created a lethargy in the Saginaw Valley. Everything was on a standstill. Curtis Emerson came from Detroit in 1846 and with Charles W. Grant purchased the abandoned East Saginaw mill and another one hundred seventy-five acres for six thousand dollars. He spent ten thousand dollars in rebuilding this mill, renaming it Emerson's Mill. In 1847 this Emerson & Eldridge Mill shipped the first cargo of clear cork pine to Albany, New York. Saginaw's clear, excellent lumber was in demand. Saginaw's lumber industry was born! From then, several mills were suddenly erected on the Saginaw River.

In 1850 the William Bros. erected another enlarged, improved sawmill next to their first one. Its circular and muley saws, lath machine, and edger had the capacity of cutting three million lathes and six million feet of lumber each season. When their first mill burned down on July 3, 1854, they suffered a nine thousand dollar loss. Everything was lost except for 100,000 board feet of lumber. Butts, Kendall & Co. also lost 500,000 board feet of lumber valued at six thousand dollars. In 1866 Geo. F. Williams built the Little Mill, with a circular saw, lath machine and edger capable of producing four million feet of lumber. Their second mill burned down on July 30, 1874. In 1874 another mill was built and was operating by the 1875 season. The Williams Bros. Mill was the oldest business organized in the Saginaw Valley.[2]

In 1850 Charles W. Grant and A.M. Hoyt opened the Blue Mill near Germain Street in East Saginaw for cutting road planks for the Genesee-Saginaw Plank Road. This mill was later purchased by Jesse Hoyt. By 1854 there were twenty-three sawmills on the river, cutting sixty million board feet of lumber. In 1857 there were forty-four mills, cutting 113,700,000 board feet of lumber. Eastern financiers were arriving daily and investing capital in new sawmills.[3]

By 1854 some of the mills up and running on the Saginaw River were: Eastman & Co., J. Pierson, Whitney & Vanston, Whiting's Mill, Jeffer's Mill, Johnson's Mill at Zilwaukee, Garrison & Bristol. In 1855 the Mershon, Whitney & Co. processed and dressed one million feet of lumber for the Chicago market. The S.T. Atwater Mill had three boilers. Warner & Co., G.W. Merrill & Beach, and Moore & Co. were expanding and enlarging their operations and processing the most lumber in the Valley. Hoyt & Whitney Mill was dressing almost thirty thousand board feet of lumber per day. If a mill burned down, it was immediately rebuilt improved and larger than the previous one.

Rafted logs are lined up as far as the eye can see at this C. K. Eddy & Son Sawmill on the west bank of the Saginaw River near where the Wickes grain elevator was later located. The Tittabawassee Boom Co. had delivered the logs and they were waiting to begin their journey into the sawmill. In the rear right of the photo are piles of finished lumber stacked up on the river docks to dry before being shipped out. This was a scene at every mill that lined the river.

In 1850 the Saginaw Valley was a primeval forest with a few scattered log cabins nearby the river banks. East Saginaw's low land and poor drainage resulted in stagnant water on the mud roads, little frog ponds and cesspools, bayous, and mosquitoes everywhere. Uncovered cellars were always full of water. East Saginaw's heterogenous population totaled three hundred with German immigrants being the majority. Cut-off tree stumps still remained on vacant lots. The Village of East Saginaw was incorporated in 1855. By 1858 its population had increased to twenty-five hundred.[4]

Salina or South Saginaw had been in existence for less than two years in May 1864, when it already had a population of eleven hundred. Since its founding there were eight deaths and six marriages. A large number of stores and houses were under construction. There already were two churches, an academy, two planing mills, three public houses, six saloons, five grocery stores, two blacksmith shops, two boot and shoe stores, two meat markets, a drug store, dry goods store, tin shop, hardware store, seven boarding houses, millinery, bakery, twenty salt blocks and sawmills, brewery, masonic lodge, seven cooper shops, and a cabinet shop. The self-sufficient town emerged almost overnight when sawmills began lining the river.[5]

The Saginaw River mills obtained their logs from the Saginaw River District composed of the counties of Tuscola, Lapeer, Genesee, Saginaw, Gratiot, Isabella, Gladwin, Clare, and Midland. Tributaries of the Saginaw and Tittabawassee Rivers were the Flint, Bad, Cass, Pine, Salt, Chippewa, Tobacco, Molasses, Cedar, Shiawassee, Rifle, and AuGres Rivers. Logs were hauled up to the banks of small streams to await the spring's high water stage. Then they were floated in lots of two to three thousand on the many rivers to the Saginaw River.[6]

The Cass River and its tributaries passed through a belt one hundred miles long and ten miles wide of densely growing cork pine. Less than twenty per cent of Michigan pine was cork pine, considered the best in the state. The clear, creamy white, light-weight wood floated easily to Saginaw sawmills. These trees were seventy to one hundred sixty years old. This pine was first sent to New York in 1847 and began the great lumber industry in the Valley.

The mature, virgin forests in central Michigan grew trees up to three hundred years old—hardwoods of oak, maple, beech, cherry, elm, white and Norway pine, hemlock, cedar, balsam, jack or scrub pine. The white pine growing on uplands and ridges towered one hundred twenty five feet to one hundred seventy feet high with trunks up to five feet in diameter. No underbrush or young pines grew under these mammoth monarchs of the forest. From 1841 to 1871 the United States Government sold large tracts of this virgin timber land to speculators for $1.25 per acre. Eastern investors came in droves to purchase large tracts of this land, to harvest the white pine, floating it to their Saginaw River sawmills, and making large fortunes. The white pine, the best building and woodworking lumber available, was harvested first. After the pine was depleted, the other hardwoods were harvested and sent to the mills. An eighty acre tract would yield about 400,000 feet of timber.

In cutting a log, a slab had to be cut first but two edges of the slab had to be removed so that the board would be the same width in its entirety. This edging process gave an ever increasing amount of scrap, sawdust, edgings, and slabs of all sizes. These seconds were cut into laths, shingles, pickets, barrel staves, hoops, and heads. Choice lumber was cut into building materials. Four-inch white pine planks were used for road building. Very small trees were used for railroad ties and fence posts for the new farms and railroads emerging in the West. One thousand feet of lumber could make up to five thousand shingles. Waste slabs and edgings were made into laths. Sawdust and waste slabs were used in salt production. In the beginning millmen dumped sawdust into the river but this interfered with navigation. When sawdust was hauled to a vacant lot, fire caused it to smoke for an entire week. However, the best solutions for this sawdust and slabs were building roads and filling up bayous and low places on mud streets with this waste. The mill yards were built up with sawdust.[7]

As the demand for window sashes, doors, wagons, buggies, roof boards, barrels, churns, pails, and furniture increased, lumber cutting methods became more efficient and productive. The heavy English gate saw cut timber slower and required manual edging on the boards. The muley saw had upright blades and continued to waste lumber, but eliminated some of the manual labor. By 1876 the band saw cut lumber thinner to permit more boards from each log and trimmed slabs from each edge, eliminating several manual steps.

The circular saw and gang saw were introduced in Michigan simultaneously and sawmills were equipped with both. The circular saw efficiently cut more than one thousand feet of lumber per hour while trimming both edges of the board. However, when the Wickes Bros. began improving the Yankee Gang Saw in 1867, lumber waste was minimized while cutting was done still more efficiently. Their saw had a series of several upright saws, which could be adjusted for various cutting sizes. After a log was passed through a circular saw four times to cant or square it, it was pushed through the gang saw cutting and edging it simultaneously. Wickes continued improving their gang saws which were sold worldwide for decades.[8]

All sawmills were erected basically alike next to the river. An average sized sawmill, salt block, cooperage, barns, offices and piling grounds covered about forty-five acres. The mill processed about twenty-five million feet of lumber, one and one-half million staves, seventy-five thousand sets of heading, and two million shingles each season. The salt wells and blocks made about fifty thousand barrels of salt. The 80' x 192' two-story wooden building had a boiler and engine room attached to it. A large chimney was used for burning slabs and sawdust as fuel to run the engines and salt wells. The seven hundred horsepower Corliss engine was fed by five boilers, each 5' x 16'. Two separate boilers fed the pony and pumping engines for salt-making.

This picturesque view of the Saginaw River sawmill shows the many buildings connected to the sawmill. The towers are the salt works wells. The rafted logs are waiting in the company's boom. Slasinski Collection

Logs were moved mechanically into the sawmill as shown on this steam-driven endless chain. Photo taken at the Gebhart & Estabrook Planing Mill in East Saginaw near Rust Bridge.

Logs were brought up the Saginaw River and stored in the company's boom until ready for use. The logs were taken from the boom by a steam-driven endless chain, the log jacker, which carried them up continuously through a door on the second floor. A steam-driven log flipper then rolled the log down an inclined plane where it was caught by a loader, and carried to one of two circular saws.

The logs were fed continuously along live rollers through several processes. After being sawed into the desired thickness, the log passed through the Wickes gang saw with its thirty-four blades. From the gang saw it traveled to the edging table machines. Edgings and slabs were cut into smaller lengths with smaller circular saws, then carried to a spout and dropped into wagons and carted to the slab piles. Larger

In the top inset the logs are in their company's boom and a worker is directing them towards the chain. In the bottom inset the logs are moved into an opening in the mill by a log jacker.

slabs were made into staves, heading, and lathes. From the edging tables, the lumber passed to the trimming tables where it was finished.

The finished lumber was run on tram cars, then drawn by horses along an elevated tramway to the piling grounds where it was stacked to dry. A mile of elevated tramway eighteen feet high circled the piling grounds located next to the river and company boom, which held up to five million feet of logs. On one side of the piling grounds was a large bayou dredged and docked from which the company did its shipping. The sawdust carrier took the sawdust from the saws direct into the fires with the surplus passing to large store houses. At night it was used to fire the furnaces used in running the pony engine for the salt works. The mill used iron wheels with two fly wheels each weighing thirty

The tramway at the Briggs & Cooper Sawmill at Ojibway Island shows the finished lumber moved from the sawmill by horses to the piling grounds where it was stacked to dry.

thousand pounds. Saws were sharpened automatically. The machines eliminated the manual lifting and handling.

An average mill employed one hundred twenty five men and sixteen horses. About two hundred fifty men worked for the company in its lumber camps in the forest, harvesting about twenty-five million feet of logs per season. Some mill owners had two or three mills since one mill could not handle their large volume of logs.[9]

The sawing season ran from mid-March until mid-December when the river was not frozen. Both banks of the river to Bay City were lined with noisy, smoking sawmills, with the sweet-smelling sawdust permeating the air the entire season. Lumber camps operated from October until mid-March when timber was harvested. Most of the

East Saginaw's Wylie Mill shows the finished lumber on the right stacked on the river bank drying, the railroad tracks which were used in late 1800's to bring the logs to the mills, and rafted lumber on the left of the tracks. Slasinski Collection

logs were brought into the Saginaw Valley by the Tittabawassee Boom Co. with the spring high waters beginning in mid-March or April and then held in booms until the sawmills requested them. Mills operated eleven or twelve hours per day, six days per week. After electricity came, some mills operated both day and night. In 1866 wages averaged $2.25 per day. This decreased to $2.00 by 1873. Before the strike in 1885, wages averaged about $1.66 per day. After the strike they averaged $1.61 per day. By 1887 workers worked ten hours per day and were paid $1.77 per day. Mill labor was obtained from the daily-arriving European immigrants, Canadians, and some shanty boys who spent winter months in lumber camps and summers in the Saginaw sawmills.

Fire was an ever constant threat to the sawmills. It was 11:10 A.M.

This Geo. Rust & Co. Sawmill shows the water barrels lined up on the roof top in case of fire. Fire was a constant threat. When a mill burned down, either the same or new owner would rebuild it. Slasinski Collection

on March 23, 1880, when clerks at the J.H. Pierson & Son's Grocery Store at the sawmill and salt works discovered smoke coming from the first floor of the store. The rear and upper part of the building were already in flames. An alarm was given. The two-story frame building facing the river had two apartments on each floor. The back store room was already filled with fire and smoke and suddenly the entire building rapidly became a sheet of roaring flames. All morning long a dredge had been at work in the bayou about five hundred feet away from the building. A railroad locomotive had been at work about one hundred fifty feet away. The wind was blowing a strong gale. A spark from the dredge or locomotive engine apparently lodged under the store's eave.

Several millmen tried in vain to save some goods from the store but were driven back by the smoke. One man fell down a flight of stairs. The fires at the sawmill were allowed to go out. Millmen attempted to put out the fire with a hose fifteen minutes later when the water works began operating. Finally Hose Co. #2 arrived. Flames spread like lightning. The store was connected to a blacksmith shop next to a drill house. By 11:40 A.M. all three buildings were one living, glowing mass of roaring, crackling fire.

Showers of burning brands of all sizes were carried across the road. A pile of 120,000 pine staves piled against the cooper shop were ignited and burned like tinder. Flames spread to the cooper shop. A band of vats filled with brine kept the fire away from the salt blocks. About seventy feet away were another drill house and the mill with its docks lined with rows of huge piles of lumber. Sawdust was afire everywhere! Everyone in the City congregated. Men swarmed everywhere. Some were stationed with pails of water on the mill roof and salt blocks, patroling the yards and lumber piles, putting out embryo conflagrations. Barrels of salt were broken open and scattered upon roofs everywhere.

Suddenly flames burst through the cooper shop, then were seized by the gale and carried to the mill and drill house. Burning brands were falling everywhere. Hose Co. #1 arrived in time to watch the cooper shop and a pile of staves being consumed. The mill had been on fire a hundred times but the fire was extinguished each time. Other mill operators—Newell Barnard, Abel Brockway, F.W. Hollister, Wm. Blesterfield, Joe Madill—had come to help extinguish fires. The entire afternoon was spent extinguishing the embers only to have another alarm given at 4:45 P.M. The remaining drill house was on fire in twenty different places. Firemen scaled the roof, cut a hole through the shingles, directing water through it. The entire sawmill and adjoining property were destroyed. Losses exceeded twenty thousand dollars and were only partially insured. Pierson would commence rebuilding a new mill immediately.[10]

Sometimes sawmill fires destroyed entire neighborhoods as the fire did at Charles E. Lee's Planing Mill on August 8, 1888. Hundreds hurried to the scene when the fire began at 4:00 P.M. Flames had already been driven to property on Washington Avenue. The mill was surrounded by flammable material. Raging flames reached forth in every direction destroying every thing in its path. Adjoining the mill was a frame building owned by Mrs. James Lewis. It was ablaze within a few minutes. The fire swept to the Lewis homestead on Hoyt & Washington Streets. The entire square bounded by Hoyt & Emily and Washington & Water was on fire. House after house melted away from the fierce heat sent out by burning lumber from the mill yard. By 6:00 P.M. the entire square was swept clean except for Geo. Moore's home on the southeast corner of the block. Firemen had been able to save it. Five other fine residences had been destroyed. It was impossible to remove any furniture since the heat drove everyone away.

Lee's mill office on Hoyt Street burned down. C.E. Lee's fine brick house on Washington Avenue shriveled and became a glowing furnace. To the north the homes of Henry Lee and Wm. Armstrong were destroyed. Furnishings from both houses were removed and carried away by drays and wagons of every kind. E.R. Phinney's home was in flames but firemen doused the roof with streams of water several times and saved it. Huge cinders fell in showers on other roofs across the avenue but were controlled. By 8:00 P.M. the fire had been controlled east of its starting point, but to the west between Water Street and the river it was raging. Flames swept rapidly through the two million feet of lumber piled fifty feet from the sawmill. Three fire tugs stationed in a slip south of the mill and the Saginaw City steamer poured streams of water on the advancing flames but to no avail. The long rows of lumber piles were reduced to heaps of glowing coals which dropped through the docks into the slips. Several times the fire tugs were on fire and were driven away. It was 10:00 P.M. before the mill fire was finally out. But the firemen stayed on until daybreak.

Several other fires had started on roofs on Warren Street but were put out with water pails or garden hoses. Every available foot of hose in the City was found and used. Several people offered their assistance. People from Bay City came to help. Chris Maier helped move the water hoses and then brought food for the weary firemen. Another lady helping people move things fell down the stairs and broke her arm. Sparks flew thick and fast igniting clothing of anyone near by. Neck collars and dresses caught on fire again and again!

Charles E. Lee suffered the most extensive damage. His loss of seventy-three thousand dollars was not insured. Nine fine residences were destroyed and dozens of homes were damaged. Total destruction exceeded ninety-five thousand dollars. Lee's planing mill was one of the oldest structures in the City. The mill had been built in 1856. The chimney had been built by Christopher Palm in 1860. This masterpiece of masonry one hundred twenty-five feet high was still standing.

Charles Lee purchased the mill in 1862 when it was used as a heading and stave factory. Lee refitted and expanded the mill several times until it was one of the most extensive plants covering all of Water Street and extending to Washington. In 1863 a saw and shingle mill was added. In 1874 a planing mill was added; a sash, door, and blind factory in

1875. In 1880 the present two-story 155' x 75' building was constructed. The property covered sixteen city lots with a six-hundred-foot river frontage. The mill employed fifty men. The sawmill had the capacity of three million feet of lumber and 700,000 lathes. Charles Lee decided not to rebuild his destroyed mill.[11]

Sawmills continually changed ownership and partners were involved in several sawmills simultaneously. John Gallagher built a mill at Center Street in South Saginaw in 1853. The mill was capable of cutting one and one-half million feet of lumber. In 1873 D.L.C. Eaton, Fred H. Potter, George L. Burrows, and L. Burrows bought the mill renaming it Eaton, Potter & Co. They improved and equipped the 100' x 150' mill with the latest machinery including two engines, six boilers, and efficient saws. They had a complete mill, salt works, salt block, drill house and employed seventy-five workmen. The mill annually produced 17,000 barrels of salt, fifteen million board feet of lumber, one million laths, 800,000 staves, 500,000 sets of heading, and a large number of pickets. The mill had the capacity of 90,000 board feet of lumber per day. Their products were sold to all markets in the East and South. D.L.C. Eaton was also a member of the Rust, Eaton & Co. and George L. Burrows & Co. Fred H. Potter was a member of the George L. Burrows & Co. George L. Burrows was involved in Burrows & Rust, Rust, Eaton & Co. and was head of his George L. Burrows & Co. banking firm.[12]

Saginaw became a major lumber town. High quality Saginaw lumber commanded good prices in Chicago, Cleveland, Buffalo, Albany, and other Midwestern ports. As the lumber production increased, the Valley's population also increased. In 1860 there was a combined population of 4,700 in the Saginaw vicinity. In 1868 Saginaw had 25,600 living in

W. C. YAWKEY & CO.,

COMMISSION DEALERS IN

Lumber, Lath and Shingles,

No. 101, Exchange Block, Genesee, cor. Water—Office, No. 13, 3d floor.

EAST SAGINAW.

Particular attention given to the Purchase, Inspection and Shipping of Lumber and Shingles from all points on Saginaw River. Address all communications, East Saginaw.

Robt. H. Weidemann,

DEALER IN

PINE LUMBER

AND SAW LOGS,

No. 101, Exchange Block, Genesee, corner Water—Office, No. 13, 3d floor.

EAST SAGINAW, MICH.

Both of these advertisements were from the 1866 directory. The lumber industry was in its heyday and newspapers and city directories were filled with advertisements for lumber products. Eddy Collection

the following towns: Saginaw City 8,000, East Saginaw 14,000, South Saginaw 2,500, Carrollton 600, and Zilwaukee 500. In 1873, there were 29,325 living in the following: East Saginaw 17,000, Saginaw City 9,000, Carrollton 1,500, Zilwaukee 1,000, Florence 550, Crow Island 275. Saginaw's total population increased to 42,867 in 1884 and 65,000 by 1890.

The total number of mills and production increased steadily. In 1868, 2,678 men were employed in eighty-nine mills, producing 457,396,225 board feet of lumber, 61,478,910 laths, 104,104,500 shingles, and 12,670,100 staves.

The entire year of 1869 was unprofitable for lumber owners. Unsold

W. J. BARTOW,

Manufacturer and Dealer In

Gang Sawed Lumber,

AND DEALER IN

PINE LANDS, LOGS, AND REAL ESTATE.

Office, Buena Vista Block,

EAST SAGINAW, MICH.

An 1870 advertisement

TEMPLE EMERY, President.   R. H. ROYS, Secretary.
    R. A. LOVELAND, Vice-President.   D. L. WHITE, Jr., Treasurer.

EMERY LUMBER CO.,

MANUFACTURERS OF

CANADIAN LUMBER.

Limits on Wahnapitae River.   Proprietors of the Log Barge "Wahnapitae."

Office, SAGINAW, MICH., East Side.   Mills, MIDLAND, ONTARIO.

This 1890 advertisement indicates that Canadian timber was already being brought to the Saginaw River and processed into lumber. Eddy Collection

lumber stacked up on mill docks. The Chicago Fire of 1871 helped reduce the Saginaw Valley's lumber supply. But the Panic of 1873 adversely affected the lumber industry and it wasn't until 1875 when the industry rebounded. In 1870, eighty-three mills employed 3,124 men and cut 576,726,606 board feet of lumber. The production peak was reached in 1882 when seventy mills cut over one billion board feet of lumber, 295,046,500 shingles, and ninety-four million laths.

Thereafter, there was a gradual decrease in mills and lumber production. By 1887, only sixty-five mills cut 779,661,265 board feet of lumber and 196,983,000 shingles. In 1891, sixty-eight mills cut 758,610,548 board feet of lumber, 222,607,250 shingles, and 153,807,800 laths. The Panic of 1893 brought several sawmills to their close. Only 2,182 men worked in the mills in 1892, cutting 708,465,027 board feet of lumber. By 1897, only 339 million board feet of lumber was cut.[13]

As Michigan pine forests became devastated, hardwoods and previously inaccessible timber were harvested and brought to Saginaw mills by railroad rather than by the rivers. As pine became scarcer, sawmills gradually declined and the huge stacks of lumber drying on the river banks grew smaller.

On January 5, 1889, A.T. Bliss and Willis Van Auken purchased the William Bros. Sawmill for $25,000. The sawmill, gang, and circular saw had a capacity of 90,000 board feet of lumber a day, a steam salt block with a capacity of two hundred barrels a day, a pan salt block, four salt wells, fifteen hundred feet of river frontage and seven hundred fifty feet of railroad front, docks, trams, and all facilities for carrying on the mill, salt and lumber yard. The oldest business in the Valley was now dissolved.[14]

In the decade from 1880 to 1890 some of the largest Saginaw Valley lumber and salt producers were: Bliss & Van Auken with an aggregation of 196,558,978 board feet of lumber and 398,157 barrels of salt; the A.T. Bliss in Carrollton with 164,775,960 board feet of lumber and

AARON P. BLISS.   **W. C. VAN AUKEN.**

BLISS & VAN AUKEN,

Saginaw, W. S., Mich.,

MANUFACTURERS AND WHOLESALE DEALERS IN

GRADED

PINE LUMBER,

HEMLOCK,

NORWAY AND HARDWOOD.

PLANING MILL IN CONNECTION.

SHIPMENTS BY RAIL OR WATER.

No Traveling Men.   **Write for Prices.**

An 1890 advertisement. Eddy Collection

443,848 barrels of salt; A. T. Bliss in Zilwaukee with 199,396,900 board feet of lumber and 489,991 barrels of salt.

In February 1900, Bliss & Van Auken added a factory for manufacturing hard maple flooring. This mill was equipped with electric power and every machine was operated by a motor. The mill operated year round for twenty-four hours a day, employed fourteen men, and turned out twenty thousand feet of hard maple daily. Since the demand for flooring was so great, the lumber to supply the mill was bought and sawed elsewhere.[15]

By the late 1890's almost every Saginaw sawmill ceased to exist. The Eddy Mill had all modern equipment installed in 1895. The power house had been built at the beginning of the lumber era and then remodeled in 1879.   In 1900 the mill ceased operations, and the machinery was sold and shipped all over the United States to be used in coal mining work. On August 30, 1905, Wickes Bros. dismantled the power house, the water tubes, boilers, one-hundred-fifty foot stack, pumps, and other apparatus and sold it to a Texas Company. This dismantling marked the end of Saginaw River sawmills. There are no remaining mills in Saginaw today. [16]

The lumber industry that was originally thought to last over one hundred years was totally depleted in less than fifty years. New lumber towns were created in its heyday, bringing increased population to Michigan. Many investors made their fortunes; several workers lost their lives. The lumber industry met its demise as swiftly as it had its beginning! New challenges awaited these lumber towns as they now fought for survival.

FOOTNOTES

1 *Saginaw Daily Courier*, 10/17/1872

2 *Saginaw Evening News*, 1/5/1889

3 *Annual Statement of the Business of Saginaw Valley and the Shore*

4 *Saginaw Evening News*, 8/19/1907

5 *East Saginaw Courier*, 5/4/1864

6 *The Industries of the Saginaws*, page 37

7 *Saginaw Weekly Enterprise*, 5/26/1870

8 *Michigan Yesterday and Today*, pages 319 – 321

9 *The Industries of the Saginaws*, pages 36 – 37

10 *Saginaw Daily Courier*, 3/24/1880

11 *Saginaw Evening News*, 8/9/1888

12 *The Industries of the Saginaws*, page 107

13 *Annual Statement of the Business of Saginaw Valley and the Shore*

14 *Saginaw Evening News*, 1/5/1889

15 *Saginaw Courier Herald*, 2/25/1900

16 *Saginaw Evening News*, 8/30/1905

BIBLIOGRAPHY

An Annual Review of the Commerce, Manufacturers and Business Interests of the Saginaw Valley, 1885

Annual Review of the Saginaw Board of Trade of the Commerce, Manufacturers and Material Resources of the Saginaw District, Courier Co. Printers and Binders, East Saginaw, 1882, 1883, 1884, 1885, 1886, 1887, 1888

Annual Statement of the Business of Saginaw Valley and the Shore, by Geo. F. Lewis and C.B. Headley, Daily Enterprise Steam Printing House, East Saginaw, 1867, 1868, 1869, 1870, 1871, 1872, 1873

Lewis, Ferris E., *Michigan Yesterday and Today*, Hillsdale Educational Publishers, Inc., 1956, pages 318 – 321

Maybee, Rolland H., *Michigan's White Pine Era*, Bureau of History, Michigan Department of State, 1988

Mills, James, *History of Saginaw County*, 1918, Volume I, pages 393 – 425

Saginaw County Historian, *Sawmills of Saginaw County*, Volume I, Issue 1, Bastian Bros & Co., 1983

The Industries of the Saginaws, J. M. Elstner & Co., East Saginaw, 1887

East Saginaw Courier, 5/4/1864, page 3, c. 1

Saginaw Daily Courier,
10/17/1872;
3/24/1880, page 2, c. 3 & 4

Saginaw Courier-Herald,
2/25/1887, page 3;
1/25/1891, page 5;
2/25/1900, page 7, c.2;
5/20/1910, page 5

Saginaw Enterprise, 9/8/1853, page 2, c. 3

Saginaw Evening News,
8/9/1888, page 6, c. 3;
1/5/1889, page 7, c. 4;
8/30/1905, page 3, c. 7;
8/19/1907, page 8

Saginaw Weekly Enterprise,
4/19/1855, page 2, c.4;
1/6/1870, page 3, c.2;
5/26/1870, page 3, c.2

VI THE
SALT BOOM

Michigan Indians had discovered and used salt for centuries. Deer licks were prevalent in several locations around the state. Early French voyageurs discovered brine currents on their journeys into Michigan. No public attention was directed to this potential source of wealth until June 1836, when Congress passed an Act to admit Michigan to the Union. The Act provided for state-owned property stating that *"all the salt springs in the state, not more than twelve with six sections of land adjoining each might be selected by the State."* On July 25, 1836, the Governor selected state lands along the Grand River, the Raisin, and Section 24 in Midland County on the Tittabawassee River about a mile from the confluence of the Salt River.

An Act of March 24, 1838 authorized State Geologist Dr. Douglas Houghton to select one of the three sites to begin boring for salt. An appropriation of three thousand dollars was granted to carry out this project. He selected the Tittabawassee River site and began boring in June. After boring for nine months the shaft reached a depth of 139' but no salt springs were tapped. Total costs were twenty-one hundred dollars. Houghton believed that salt springs could be tapped at 600', but the State suspended operations at this time. All further attempts and experiments in pursuing this salt resource were abandoned.[1]

Dr. George A. Lathrop of East Saginaw became interested in Dr. Houghton's experiments. In 1854 salt springs were found in Saginaw County, in several places on the Cass River and in Tuscola County. S. Gordon took a pint of water from the Tittabawassee River to Dr. M.J. Plessner of Saginaw City. His chemical analysis showed one hundred fifty grains of good tasting salt with no bitterness, some iron, sulphate of soda and muriate of lime. Dr. Lathrop was convinced that there were many saliferous rocks in Michigan, that a vast salt basin actually existed in Michigan, and that the center of the salt basin was in the Saginaw Valley. He believed that Michigan salt brine was stronger than that in Onandaga Springs, New York, where the state owned, developed, and operated the largest salt manufacturing works in the country. He believed that boring for salt at Green Point where all rivers joined to form the Saginaw River would require about 600' depth to tap salt springs. Further up the river, drilling to 1,000' might be necessary.

In 1859 the State Legislature introduced a bill to appropriate ten thousand dollars to develop salt springs in the Grand River Valley. Dr. George A. Lathrop presided at an emergency meeting of both Saginaws' leading business men on January 26, 1859 at Charles R. Mott's office. A committee drafted a petition to present to the Legislature with the aid of Saginaw Senator James Birney. As a result, the original bill for Grand River Valley development was dismissed. On February 13, 1859, the Legislature passed a new Act which exempted from taxation all property used in connection with salt works and granted a bounty of ten cents per bushel on all salt manufactured. This equated to fifty cents a barrel.[2]

Immediately the East Saginaw Salt Manufacturing Co. was organized with capital of fifty thousand dollars and two thousand shares. On

March 30, 1859, the stock was offered for sale and by April 1, a total of twenty-one shareholders had purchased the entire amount. Jesse Hoyt was the largest holder with one hundred eighty shares. There were fourteen holders, all leading business men, with one hundred twenty shares each, among them being W.L.P. Little, W.L. Webber, G.A. Lathrop, H.C. Potter, and W.F. Glasby. Two shareholders owned forty shares each, two twenty shares each, and two ten shares each. Articles of Association were signed on April 16, 1859, with Dr. G.A. Lathrop as president, W.L.P. Little treasurer, and W.L. Webber secretary. Since Jesse Hoyt owned land in the best saline district in East Saginaw, he made a conditional sale of his ten acres in northern East Saginaw. If no springs were found, the sale would be annulled.

George W. Merrill and S.R. Kirby studied the salt manufacturing works in New York. By June 16, 1859, the East Saginaw Salt Manufacturing Co. had already erected the buildings and towers necessary to begin boring, purchased an engine and boilers, and engaged several men in making drills and other machinery. The company believed they would need to bore only 400' deep since Saginaw was in the center of a great salt basin.

By August the company's work was progressing well. Their first well had been abandoned at ninety-two feet when a drill broke and couldn't be retrieved. Another well was started about two feet from the first one. At a fifty-foot depth, gravel and very pure white sandstone were discovered. The well was sunk from five to eleven feet per day. By September 1, the well had been bored to a depth of 220' and by September 22, it reached a depth of 350'. A large volume of water continually rose to the top and floated off with such force that no pumping was needed. The water contained eleven per cent salt. The company's salt experiment was successful.[3]

The first well was bored to a depth of 647'. Another well was bored to 806' with salinometer at eighty degrees and kettle blocks were added. Both wells were completed in April 1860, but manufacturing did not begin until July 1860. When the company opened its salt blocks to the public on July 4, throngs of people from both Saginaws came all day long. In August the company built a dock to accommodate several large vessels, built additional buildings and added two blocks with fifty kettles each. Dr.H.C. Potter superintended the salt manufacturing. In 1860 the salt works manufactured four thousand barrels.

The East Saginaw Salt Manufacturing Co.'s *"salt bulletin"* triggered an electric response in the community. Within ten months of the state-offered bounty, salt works were established at Saginaw City Manufacturing Co., the Bay City Co., Portsmouth Co., and three works at Carrollton. By December 31, 1861, there were eight salt manufacturing companies with eighteen blocks. Wells were generally bored to depths ranging from 540' to 850'. Further up the river at Portsmouth and Bay City the wells were not sunk as deep. At the mouth of the river, wells were bored about 600' deep and produced a strong inexhaustible brine current.[4]

Michigan's salt bounty was more liberal and encouraging than New York's plan. Since the New York saline district had been state owned since 1779, the state furnished all equipment. Saginaw's salt enterprise was so successful that the Legislature of 1861 modified its original Act, granting a bounty of ten cents for each barrel and ceasing all bounties when $1,000 was paid. Until the Act was repealed the state was ordered to pay the East Saginaw Salt Manufacturing Co. $3,174 in bounties.

By December 1862, forty salt wells were in operation and just as many more were under construction. Towers and shafts were located all along both sides of the river from its mouth to a distance of twenty-two miles. Others were in progress on the Cass and Tittabawassee Rivers and at Flushing. All the wells produced a daily aggregate of 2,000 barrels worth about $6,000. All the Saginaw Valley manufacturers produced a total of 125,000 barrels in 1861 and 243,000 barrels in 1862. This new resource provided new jobs to several men, stimulating trade and industry. There were barrels to be made, wood to be chopped and hauled, machinery and kettles to be provided, vats, blocks, and river docks to be built, and salt to be shipped.[5]

Real estate prices all along the river escalated dramatically. Salt works, wells, and blocks were located on the river which was ideal for shipping. River front and nearby woodland property all commanded good prices. Saginaw's salt experiment created as much, if not more, excitement than the oil wells in Pennsyslvania. Investors came daily to the Saginaws prospecting for salt. More than one million dollars had already been invested in the Valley's salt operations.

By February 1864, there were thirty-three salt works in operation in Zilwaukee, Carrollton, Florence, Saginaw City, East Saginaw, and Salina with another twenty-five in Kawkawlin, Bangor, Salzburg, Woodside, Bay City, Portsmouth, and on the Cass River. Salina or South Saginaw near the river's mouth had the most with twelve companies. Most of these works were established on one-acre parcels, with some ranging up to a two thousand acre tract. Each one had one or two blocks each containing from one hundred to four hundred sixteen kettles. Their wells were bored to depths ranging from 700' to 1030'. Each of the salt works manufactured from 3,500 to 13,000 barrels of salt yearly. From $3,000 to $250,000 had been invested in each of the works.

This sawmill shows the several salt well towers which pumped up the salt brine, the smokestack chimney, and the salt kettles. To the right is stacked lumber drying in the sun. A logging train is running down the middle. Slasinski Collection

All salt works were built alike. After a river location was selected, a 16' x 30' drill house with a fifty-foot tower was built. This building held a boiler, engine, and forge. Then a three-foot long chisel-shaped steel drill was used to bore the well. Wells were bored upon contract by men who engaged only in this business. Prices varied from $1.50 to $2.00 per foot with some wells costing from $2,000 to $3,000. Sand was removed during the drilling, and tubing was inserted until it penetrated the saliferous rock. Depending on locations, well depths varied from 500' to 1200'.

Since the brine from every new salt well was weak, a sufficient quantity of brine and fresh water had to be pumped out until the brine reached the proper strength. Depending on its locality, a well would pump from twelve to twenty gallons of brine per minute. A good well would fill a 20' x 30' x 6' cistern with a capacity of 25,000 gallons in twenty hours. Cisterns were built of three inch plank, keyed and caulked together to prevent leakage and elevated on piling or timbers to allow the settled brine to flow through three inch wooden supply pipes to the blocks. The brine was controlled by gates. All salt brine contained iron. If the brine were boiled or evaporated with the iron present, the salt would have a very red color. Settling brine was necessary. A tight box large enough to hold a barrel of water was placed on top of the cistern. Fresh burnt lime and water were added to this barrel. This mixture was sprinkled over, then mixed into the brine. The iron precipitated with the lime and settled to the bottom of the cistern. After the brine had settled for forty-eight hours, it was clear and ready for boiling.

Salt was manufactured by evaporation of the brine. This was done by three methods: boiling in kettles or pans, using the exhaust steam from the sawmills, and using solar evaporation. The salt works connected to a sawmill would utilize all three methods in its salt making. Refuse from the sawmill was used for boiling. Salt works operating without a sawmill would employ a method using materials that were inexpensive to obtain. Almost all salt manufacturing was done in conjunction with a sawmill to utilize waste materials and reduce production costs.

A wooden 140' x 45' x 50' building elevated eighteen feet housed a kettle block. Fifty to sixty kettles each having a capacity from one hundred to one hundred twenty gallons were set close together in two rows three feet over fire arches extending from the furnace to the chimney. The well-cleaned kettles were filled with brine. While the brine boiled, scum was continually removed. Salt crystals would eventually form on the top and then fall to the kettle bottom. After the brine was boiled one third down, salt was dipped out with a ladle, and thrown into a basket next to the kettle. All chlorides were allowed to drain off for three hours. The remaining brine and bitter water in the kettle were discarded. The kettle was then rinsed clean and refilled with brine to start the process anew. Each kettle was boiled up to twelve hours both day and night. Four men—two boilers and two firemen—took turns working twelve hour shifts. A good kettle block produced seventy-five barrels of salt every twenty-four hours.

Pan blocks were various sized buildings erected to hold pans, settlers, and salt bins. The plate iron boiler pans were 90' long x 40' high x 15' wide, and 1' deep. The crystallized salt was raked to a side, lifted out with a shovel and placed on draining boards for several hours. The brine boiled more rapidly in these pans. Waste wood slabs were used for fuel. After draining, the salt was shoveled into barrows and taken to the store bins for further drainage.

Steam evaporation produced the greater portion of Michigan salt. A steam block was generally 150' x 122' and elevated 52'. Inside settlers were 150' x 11' x 1' deep. Brine was first pumped into outside settlers where it was allowed to partially settle. It then was drawn into the inside steam settlers where it was heated by steam pipes and brought to a saturation point just before salt crystals formed. It then was allowed to settle until all iron drained to the bottom. The brine was drawn into grainers where salt crystals fell to the bottom. Stirring the brine made the crystals fine. Evaporation was allowed to continue for twenty-four hours with a temperature of 175 degrees. Then salt was removed with shovels and put on draining boards for twenty-four hours. Salt dried in bins for two weeks before it was prepared for shipping.[6]

Solar evaporation required a series of covers or wooden vats elevated three feet off the ground on wooden supports. Each cover had a moveable roof which was run off or on according to the weather. When storm clouds hovered, *RUN COVERS, BOYS* would be heard as men rushed to replace roofs on the covers. The brine was pumped from the cisterns into the settling covers where oxygen absorbed some of the iron. As soon as salt crystals formed, this "salt pickle" was drawn into draining vats where salt continued to crystallize in the cover bottoms. Salt pickle was removed continually to allow good salt to continue forming. Dry, clear, hot weather was essential for this process, which took six to eight weeks. Three crops were gathered in mid-July, early September, and end of October. The September crop was generally the best since the salt was coarser. The salt was removed with a rake, washed in the pickle, then shoveled into draining tubs where it remained for fourteen days before being ready for packing.[7]

Michigan salt was graded as follows: (1) No. 1 Salt—*fine* for general and all family purposes, *packers* for meat and fish, *solar* or C for coarse and F for *fine*. (2) No. 2 Salt—all that rejected in No. 1 inspection was used for salting stock, hay, hides. (3) Dairy Salt used for dairy herds. (4) Agricultural Salt used for fertilizing purposes.[8]

As soon as Michigan salt found its way into the Northwest markets as early as 1862, its powerful New York rival began competing against it. Saginaw production costs averaged about $1.50 per barrel and Onondaga's total production costs were thirty-four cents per barrel. To compete with Saginaw salt, New York sold its salt for $2.35 per barrel in the East, but undersold its salt in the Midwest markets for $1.00 per barrel. The average price for Saginaw salt continued to decrease: in

An 1870 advertisement Eddy Collection

1866 it was $1.80 per barrel; in 1868 it increased to $1.85. But in 1871 it decreased to $1.46; in 1873 to $1.37; in 1876 to $1.05; in 1879 to $1.02. In 1880 it dropped to 75 cents per barrel.[9]

In 1862 Dr. Potter stated there should be an authorized rigid salt inspection to guarantee unity among all Saginaw manufacturers in packing and branding, to provide reliable and reasonable transportation to all markets, and to keep manufacturers from competing against each other. Manufacturers needed to work together to build up a distinctive trade. As early as 1866 Saginaw manufacturers realized they had to unite together to protect their future interests. Saginaw Valley salt gained its reputation from its quality. Quality varied with each manufacturer but Saginaw salt had to be uniform, and this could only be accomplished with inspection laws. Just one inferior salt shipment would damage Saginaw's entire reputation. Oversupply would also decrease prices. Dr. S.S. Garrigues came to Saginaw in 1862, became involved in salt quality, and then was appointed Saginaw's salt inspector in 1865. State inspection laws were not mandated until 1869. The Michigan Salt Association was organized in 1876 with four-fifths of all state manufacturers joining. The Association's principal office was located in East Saginaw with W.R. Burt as its president.[10]

Saginaw salt won national honors. When Burnham & Still exhibited their salt in the Cincinnati exposition in 1873, they received a silver medal and diploma. In 1873 Saginaw salt was sold to markets in Chicago, Milwaukee, Toledo, Cleveland, and Sandusky. The Michigan Salt Association regulated, marketed, and distributed Saginaw salt nationwide.

All Saginaw salt was packed in two hundred eighty pound barrels made of pine or oak staves and headings from the sawmills' refuse

An 1890 advertisement Eddy Collection

lumber. Sawmills made their own barrels in cooper shops connected to the salt blocks. Saginaw's superior oak barrels were in demand worldwide. Between 1860 and 1865 three million barrels were shipped to New York, then to England, Germany, France, and Spain and used for wine casks. The average cost of a salt barrel was twenty-two cents with labor costs ranging from nine cents to twelve cents per barrel. In 1870 there had been numerous strikes in Saginaw among barrel makers. At this time several Saginaw manufacturers met and established uniform escalating prices and wages ranging from nine cents to twelve cents per barrel depending on the season in which it was made. [11]

Saginaw Valley's many salt works had various beginnings. The C & E TenEyck's Shingle Mill was originally operated as a stave yard before being converted into a sawmill and shingle factory. The Salt Well was 728' deep and had a capacity of ninety-two barrels per day. Sixty men were employed for the entire operation.

The Millard & Sweet Mill was built in 1851. Ownership changed often, being sold to J. E. Earle, Curtis & King, and Gordon Corning. In 1871 Alex Gebhart and John S. Estabrook purchased it. The first salt well was bored in 1876 at 790', the second in 1877 at 787', and the third in 1880 at 774'. The salt works made 135 barrels of salt daily, with four cisterns, two steam settlers, six grainers, using steam power evaporation. The salt works investment costing $22,000 was a large operation, and employed fifteen men.

In his Salt Works Jesse Hoyt personally supervised the first well built in 1860 at 745', the second well in 1873 at 700', and the third well in 1874 at 764'. Sixteen cisterns held 100 barrels of brine each and were arranged in six blocks. Solar evaporation was used with 497 covers manufacturing 600 barrels per week. The cooper shop made 100 barrels a day at a cost of twenty-three cents per barrel. All the salt was shipped in bulk to Chicago to be sold to stock yard operators.

Saginaw Valley's salt production varied yearly. Total production was 125,000 barrels in 1861. Production increased to 755,015 barrels in 1871. But in 1872 it decreased to 715,316. The years preceding The Panic of 1873 had an adverse impact on Michigan's lumber industry. The entire year of 1869 had been an unprofitable year for Michigan lumbermen. The processed lumber far exceeded its demand. Both lumber and salt production slumped beginning in 1869. Processed lumber remained unsold stacked at lumber yards. When the demand for lumber fell, salt production also decreased since lumber waste was used for manufacturing. The Chicago Fire of 1871 helped to pull Saginaw out of its recession. The great demand for lumber and building materials in Chicago increased Saginaw's lumber and salt production. In 1873, 810,495 barrels of salt were produced. By 1875 it had increased to 970,444 barrels. The number of staves manufactured also varied. In 1871 there were 3,820,000. In 1873 there were 9,568,898, but in 1875 there were only 3,113,721. Salt production was at its peak in 1886 when 1,213,764 barrels were manufactured by fifty-two salt works with forty-five steam blocks. Thereafter, there was a gradual decline in both salt works and production.[12]

The salt industry provided employment to a large number of men. The total number of men employed in the industry varied from six hundred to over eight hundred yearly. An additional six hundred men worked on loading vessels when salt was in its full production. The number of men working in a salt works varied from two to over sixty men. The average company employed thirteen men in its salt works and produced at least 13,000 barrels of salt yearly. A large company such as the East Saginaw Salt Manufacturing Co. employed seventy-five men and produced about 48,000 barrels per year. In 1873 men's wages averaged two dollars per day, but there was a gradual decline in daily wages after that. [13]

During the 1890's Michigan's lumber industry became exhausted. Available supplies of timber were depleted. With the gradual decline in lumber manufacturers there was a corresponding decline in salt manufacturers. In 1891 there were ninety-five lumber manufacturers and thirty-four salt manufacturers. During The Panic of 1893 only fifty-five lumber and twenty-eight salt manufacturers remained. By 1895 there were forty-nine lumber and twenty-six salt manufacturers. Only twenty-eight lumber and eighteen salt makers remained in 1897. Salt prices decreased significantly. In 1890 the price was 55 1/10 cents per barrel. By 1893 it dropped to 44 7/10 cents per barrel. In 1895 it was 48 9/10 cents per barrel. In 1895, 479,887 barrels of salt were still inspected in Saginaw. Without the sawmill exhaust steam and waste products, salt manufacturing became unprofitable. Any remaining salt works obtained their steam from the new cheap slack coal which was just recently being mined in the Saginaw Valley.[14]

By 1898 Saginaw Lumber & Salt Co. remained the largest lumber and salt manufacturer in the Valley. The company had been incorporated in 1881 with $100,000 capital. The company was located on fifty acres on Crow Island. President R.A. Loveland advertised Saginaw to the outside world. Shipment of their products was by rail all over the United States.

Nine leading Saginaw business men incorporated the Saginaw Plate Glass Co. in 1899 with Frederick W. Carlisle as president and William J. Wickes as vice-president. The company utilized the Valley's natural

SECTION OF SETTLING TANKS, SALT WORKS OF
SAGINAW PLATE GLASS COMPANY

resources in its plate glass manufacturing. There was a new ready plate glass market. The great demand for plate glass was fostered by the automobile and furniture industries. In 1905 the company added a modern salt block to utilize the plant's exhaust steam. Everything in this automatic salt making plant was made of concrete and steel instead of wood. There were twelve wells ranging from 700' to 800' deep, concrete settling tanks, twelve grainers, Wilcox automatic rakes and electric conveyors. The company burned 250 tons of coal daily for its plate glass manufacturing and the exhaust steam was used in the salt manufacturing. In 1911 a chemical plant was added to process the calcium chloride waste to be used for the refrigerating and cold storage businesses and for roads to help settle dust. In the 1800's this waste had

HILLS OF SALT IN HUGE WAREHOUSE, DRYING OUT FOR PACKING
IN BARRELS, SAGINAW PLATE GLASS COMPANY

been dumped into the river. In 1913 the plate glass plant was expanded, and 350 men worked in its operation. Thirty men worked in the salt operation, making 1,000 barrels of salt daily. The medium salt was shipped in bulk by railroad cars to Central and Southern states.

In 1905 there were sixteen Saginaw lumber and only seven salt manufacturers—Bliss & Van Auken, Crescent Salt Co., C.K Eddy, D. Hardin, Mershon, Schuette & Parker, Michigan Salt Association, and Saginaw Lumber & Salt Co. In 1906 Saginaw produced a total of 9,936,802 barrels of salt.

In June 1912, the D. Hardin Salt Block was torn down. Conrad Kull originally built the block in 1862 on S. Hamilton, manufacturing kettle salt there for decades. It was one of Saginaw City's most productive wells. Ownership passed to N & A Barnard and then to Brand &

Hardin. The Salt Block had been rebuilt several times, the last time being in 1899. Salt was made until 1908. The high cost of production and low salt prices made it unprofitable to continue. The lumber was preserved, and the Salt Block was converted into a bean elevator.[15]

In 1914 a total of 11,670,976 barrels of salt were produced. In 1916 only six lumber manufacturers and two salt makers—Bliss & Van Auken and Strable Lumber & Salt—still remained. Strable Lumber & Salt closed in the 1930's. Carrollton's Saginaw Salt Products began business after this but closed in 1944, bringing Saginaw's inexhaustible salt industry to its conclusion.

FOOTNOTES

1 *Saginaw Daily Courier*, 1/16/1880

2 *Ibid*

3 *East Saginaw Courier*, 6/16, 8/18, and 9/1/1859

4 *Saginaw Courier*, 12/16/1862

5 *Ibid*

6 *East Saginaw Courier*, 5/31/1865

7 *Saginaw Daily Courier*, 8/2/1870

8 *Annual Statement of the Business of Saginaw Valley and the Shore*

9 *Saginaw Daily Courier,* 5/26/1870

10 *Ibid*,1/16/1880

11 *Annual Statement of the Business of Saginaw Valley and the Shore*

12 *Ibid*

13 *Saginaw Daily Courier*, 4/30/1870

14 *East Saginaw and Saginaw City Directories*

15 *Saginaw Courier Herald*, 6/11/1912

BIBLIOGRAPHY

Annual Review of the Saginaw Board of Trade of the Commerce, Manufacturers and Material Resources of the Saginaw District, Courier Co. Printers and Binders, East Saginaw, 1882, 1883, 1884, 1885, 1886, 1887, 1888

Annual Statement of the Business of Saginaw Valley and the Shore, by Geo. F. Lewis and C.B. Headley, Daily Enterprise Steam Printing House, East Saginaw, 1867, 1868, 1869, 1870, 1871, 1872, 1873

East Saginaw and Saginaw City Directories, Western Publishing Co., Chicago, 1866 – 1872; R.L. Polk & Co., Detroit, 1876 – 1897

Mills, James, *History of Saginaw County*, 1918, Volume I, pages 426 – 445

East Saginaw Courier,
6/16, 8/18, and 9/1/1859, page 3, c. 1
2/9 and 2/23/1860, page 2 and page 1
3/29/1860, page 2, c. 2
6/27/1861, page 2
5/20/1862, page 1
12/16/1862, page 1, c.4
2/10/1864, page 2, c. 1- 6
12/28/1864, page 1, c.7 –8
5/31/1865, page 2
10/4/1865, page 3

Saginaw Courier, 9/16/1862, page 1, c. 5

Saginaw Courier Herald, 6/11/1912, page 3, c. 3

Saginaw Daily Courier,
4/30, 5/2, and 5/26/1870, page 2
8/2/70, page 2, c. 3
11/18/1870, page 2
1/16/1880, page 1, c. 3 – 5

Saginaw Evening News,
10/26/1887, page 7, c. 3,
6/7/1889, page 1, c. 3

Saginaw Weekly Enterprise,
9/22/1859, page 2, c.1
8/23/1860, page 2, c. 5
12/4/1862, page 3, c. 1
2/1/1866, page 2 & page 3

VII Taming
The Swamp

Visitors to the Saginaw Valley were discouraged from coming since the entire Valley had a reputation of a worthless, mosquito-infested swamp, habitable only by wild animals, bullfrogs, and insects. Almost all travelers and settlers came down with swamp ague. The Chippewa Indians found the Saginaw Valley a beautiful, fertile country. The river banks rolled with luxurious, beautiful flower gardens growing profusely with wild morning glories, roses, and a variety of flowers. Wild fruits and shrub berries—plums, cherries, grapes, whortleberries, blackberries, black and red raspberries, currants, gooseberries, cranberries—grew in profusion on the bottom lands and along the many streams. Wild rice and marsh reeds grew in abundance choking the many waterways. A rich stand of walnut, linden, lynn, maple, and pine lined the banks and prairies of the Saugenah River. Grape vines laden with abundant fruit wrapped themselves about the many trees. Clumps of apple trees grew sporadically along the river banks. Every year the spring floods overflowed the banks renewing the fertility of the alluvial bottom lands. The wet prairies were covered with towering marsh grasses.

Indian villages and camp sites were found throughout the territory draining into the Saugenah River. The Indians frequently roamed and moved their camps during the hunting seasons. But during the winter and spring seasons they lived in their villages. While the men engaged in hunting, fishing, meetings, and raids, the squaws did all the labor and farming. With crude instruments the women tilled the soil, planted the corn and beans, and harvested the crops. The women and young maidens gathered and preserved the abundant fruits and berries.

This Indian agriculture was a simple, self-sustaining endeavor. To clear a patch of woodland, the Indians merely cut a ring of bark from each tree. After the trees died, a patch of fertile ground remained. Using wooden hoes the women scraped the earth into hills and planted corn seeds among the tree stumps. Maize was planted in hills in an irregular manner instead of in rows. Maize grew unaided in the warm, fertile soil. The women drove the blackbirds from the patch, pulled the weeds, and gathered the harvest without tools. They pounded the parched corn, hung it in wigwams to dry, and stored it in pits or caches.

Early white pioneers found evidence of this simple Indian agriculture in the remains of several of the Indian villages. Camp sites and burial mounds contained implements, storage caches, and blades. Cultivated patches of land were found at Crow Island, Melbourne Fields, Hickory Place (Castle Building site), Mowbray Village (Water Works site), Green Point, several places along the Tittabawassee River, and Black Birds' Village in Freeland.

The 1830's pioneers from New York believed that they could farm as they had back East, by sowing seed on raw, sandy soil, only to find their crops devoured by blackbirds, crows, and grubs. Most of these pioneers were migratory, continually moving westward to more pleasant areas.

However, there were some early settlers who successfully conquered the land. In 1833 Albert Miller used oxen to plow thirty acres of prairie land at Green Point. That summer the blackbirds nearly destroyed his corn crop, eating sixty bushels per acre, and leaving him only the corn butts which he used to fatten his hogs. His cows were pastured in the woods across the river from his cabin. While crossing the river daily to milk them, he caught fish for his dinner enroute . His hogs kept the many rattlesnakes away from his clearing. When Charles Lull came to Spaulding Township in 1833, he was the first farmer to raise wheat on his eighty acres. He eventually bought one hundred acres in Bridgeport and farmed there until his death in 1885.

In 1832 James McCormick settled his family on 150 acres of cleared land on an abandoned Indian field in Bridgeport. He renamed it the Garden of Eden. The land produced excellent crops. In one year he sold 1,000 bushels of corn to the American Fur Company. Meanwhile James Fraser settled his family on sixty acres on the Tittabawassee River near Paine's Junction. He produced seventy bushels of corn per acre, raised sixty -pound pumpkins, produced abundant plums, apples, and peaches, and then distributed tubs of the fruit to his neighbors.

Saginaw's poor natural drainage, travel difficulties, and limited markets delayed agricultural development. Subsistence farming existed before the lumber industry reached its peak. Early pioneers lived in their crude log cabins in scattered clearings. Their diets were sparse— boiled potatoes, Johnny-cake, roasted wild meats, flour gravy. They worked long hours at hard manual labor and endured a scarcity of food and other provisions. They worked with their oxen in the woods and lumber camps in the winter, then cleared and cultivated their own land in the summer. Before ground could be cultivated, trees were felled, brush cut, logs burned, and soil broken with oxen and crude plows. Crops harvested were used for their own and their animals' consumption. Extras were sold as animal feed for city horses.[1]

Congress had passed laws in 1820 permitting settlers to purchase

CHARLES L. ORTMANN,

DEALER IN

LOGS, LUMBER, PINE AND FARMING LANDS,

Office Wilkin's Building, Genesee St., opp. Bancroft House,

EAST SAGINAW, - MICH.

————————

Prompt attention given to purchase and Sale of Land, paying Taxes, Estimating of Timber, examining

PINE AND FARMING LANDS,

Colionists, actual Settlers, and Emigrants furnished with Land Descriptions and Information free of charge.

An 1873 advertisement. Eddy Collection

eighty acres at $1.25 per acre. However, before putting the land on the market, the country was surveyed into townships, each six miles square. Each township was subdivided into sections, one mile square with thirty-six sections in a township. Each section was 640 acres. Each section was subdivided into quarter sections of 160 acres; then further divided into quarter sections of forty acres each. Section Sixteen of each township was set aside for public schools.

David Geddes began living in Section 21 of Thomastown in 1861. He cleared thirteen acres the first year, planting eight acres of wheat, harvesting twenty-eight bushels to the acre. The following year he cleared another seven acres, planting wheat, harvesting thirty-four bushels per acre. He continued clearing land each year until by 1877 he had cleared and cultivated 160 acres. He planted wheat, corn, oats, hay, potatoes, beets, turnips, carrots, barley, apple trees, pears, plums, grapes, cherries, strawberries, currants, gooseberries. His grain produced 45 bushels per acre, corn 183 bushels per acre, vegetables 1200 bushels per acre, and his fruit trees about 1,000 bushels total. He raised fifteen head of cattle and ten horses.[2]

Jesse Hoyt purchased 130 acres in Buena Vista Township in 1876. His agent, W.J. Bartow, cultivated the clay loam soil which previously had white oak, beech, maple, basswood, and elm harvested. No fertilizers were used. In 1876 Bartow harvested 700 bushels of wheat and 700 bushels of oats from sixty acres. He removed the stumps from the remaining land and cultivated it in 1877. He harvested 250 bushels of winter wheat from six acres, 900 bushels of spring wheat from fifty-six acres, 1600 bushels of oats from thirty acres, 1600 bushels of potatoes from ten acres, fifteen tons of Hungarian grass from eight acres, 2100 bushels of corn from seventeen acres, and 1500 bushels of carrots from three acres.   Former timber soil was proving to be extremely productive.[3]

Saginaw County had 18,048 acres of improved, slashed land in 1860. By 1870, there were 33,383 improved, slashed acres. Although there were scattered dedicated farmers throughout the area, most of the serious farming was found in the industrious German farming colonies at Frankenmuth, Frankentrost, Frankenlust, and Amelith. More agricultural development occurred from 1870 to 1874 than it had in the preceding twenty years.

The lumber industry was now in its heyday and opened up more land and created new markets in and out of Saginaw for its agricultural products. Thousands of European immigrants were coming to America during "The Great Atlantic Migration." Recruitment efforts by

FLINT AND PERE MARQUETTE RAILWAY LANDS.

The ENTIRE LAND GRANT of this company unsold, consisting of about **280,000 Acres** is offered for sale.

PINE LANDS!

Over 900,000.000 Feet well located, mainly on the Rivers leading into Lake Michigan. The numerous streams and small lakes surrounded with pine timber along the line west of Reed City, offer the best of locations for mills, where logs can be held safely free of expense and free from the annoyance of Boom Companies. The Railroad direct to East Saginaw and Toledo offers the best source of supplies, and a never failing market for Lumber, Shingles, &c.. which may be delivered anywhere on the line.

FARMING LANDS,

As good as any in the world are to be found in abundance, and will be sold on the most favorable terms to actual settlers. Some level and heavily timbered with

OAK, BEECH, MAPLE, &C.

Some rolling with

BEECH, MAPLE ROCK ELM, &C.

In fact, every variety of timber, soil and surface can be found.
The Railroad is complete to Reed City (T. 17. N R. 10 West) and there is only 48 Miles to reach Ludington on Lake Michigan. This will be constructed as fast as the work can economically be done. Cheap Land and Railroad Facilities are seldom offered together. and those who wish to secure homes will do well to apply early and take choice selections.

TERMS OF SALE.

One-Fourth down, in all cases—and balance may be paid in three equal annual payments. Timber Lands must be paid for, before being cut. FARMING LANDS for actual settlement will be sold on payment of one-fourth cash and the balance in five equal annual payments.

Interest at the rate of seven per cent. on all unpaid balances, to be paid annually.

All Contracts and Notes are made payable at Merchants' National Bank, in East Saginaw.

Apply in person or by mail to

WM. L. WEBBER,
Land Commissioner.

Land Office at East Saginaw, Mich.

An 1872 Advertisement. Eddy Collection

Michigan immigration agents in New York and by Max R. Allardt in Bavaria, Germany brought thousands of German peasants to Saginaw, seeking their own land.

The railways began selling land to settlers. In East Saginaw Attorney William L. Webber was the Land Commissioner, serving as the agent for the Flint & Pere Marquette Railway Company. As the lumber industry progressed in Michigan, former timber land was sold to farmers. Communities with houses, farms, schools, and churches developed rapidly across mid-Michigan from Ludington to Saginaw. In purchasing farm land, one-fourth of the price had to be paid down, and the remaining three to five equal payments were paid annually with interest at seven per cent. Timber land had to be paid in full before timber was harvested. Michigan farm land was selling for $14.16 per acre while twenty-two other Western states were selling land at $9.61 per acre.[4]

The Flint & Pere Marquette Railway advertised its Michigan pine and farming lands extensively in the East. Throughout Michigan settlers bought land from lumber companies, from the railroad land grants, from sections previously reserved for schools, or homesteaded under the Homestead Act of 1862. Saginaw County's agricultural produce and land doubled in production and value during the next five years.

Saginaw County had 182,069 total acres of farm land with 85,955 acres in improved, slashed land in 1879. There were 2,294 county farms with the average size farm being 79.37 acres. The German farming communities had the greatest acreage and farms as follows: Frankenmuth with 9,944 acres and 218 farms; Blumfield (Frankentrost) with 7,059 acres and 173 farms; Kochville (Frankenlust and Amelith) with 9,271 acres and 193 farms. Eastern townships and those with the major rivers also had the greatest acreage and farms as follows: Taymouth with 8,507 acres and 122 farms; Saginaw with 6,724 acres and 134 farms; Thomas with 5,224 acres and 142 farms; Birch Run with 6,081 acres and 194 farms; Bridgeport with 6,636 acres and 176 farms; Tittabawassee with 7,982 acres and 249 farms. Transportation on plank roads and rivers and streams was more accessible in all these townships.

The county's western and southern townships were not yet as developed. Their cleared acreage and farms were as follows: Carrollton with 503 acres and ten farms; James with 1,083 acres and 28 farms; Lakefield with 245 acres and 17 farms; Swan Creek with 788 acres and 40 farms; Spaulding with 1,628 acres and 47 farms; Albee with 904 acres and 45 farms; Buena Vista with 3,200 acres and 74 farms; Chapin with 1,658 acres and 79 farms; St. Charles with 1,791 acres and 60 farms.

The fertile river bottom lands were good grain producing areas. In 1879 county farms raised almost 21,000 acres of wheat, 7,137 acres of corn, 11,093 acres of oats, 16,000 acres of hay, 2200 acres of potatoes, 950 acres of peas, 500 acres of barley. Other leading crops were clover seed, apples, grapes, cherries, currants, plums, berries. There were almost 4800 horses, 6800 milch cows, 8600 other cattle, 7800 hogs, and 9000 sheep.[5]

The vast swamp in South Saginaw's Albee and St. Charles Townships was once the bottom of Glacial Lake Saginaw. It laid south and east of the Flint and Shiawassee Rivers. Annual floods left a six-foot watermark on trees, and through millions of years deposited salt, gypsum, and organic matter. The seven-foot high marsh grass was blown flat by winter storms, decomposing, enriching this muck land. Although many considered it a large waste land, buggy manufacturer Harlan P. Smith believed that this vast swamp could be reclaimed and serve as a productive farming operation. In 1885 Smith and attorneys Charles H. Camp and George B. Brooks bought 10,000 acres of this muck land and intended to drain it. They asked for bids to tackle the mammoth task.

German-born brewer Michael Schrems won the contract to dig the drainage ditches. If the job were completed in eight years, he would receive a buggy as a bonus. Schrems immediately set up a camp at the village of Alicia. He hired a crew of fifty to one hundred local farmers who lived at this camp. He also hired a foreman and a cook, Mrs. McCarthy. Schrems himself lived at his home in Saginaw and continued to operate his saloon in East Saginaw, but he made a couple trips weekly to Alicia with provisions and other supplies.

Reclaiming this vast swamp was a slow, arduous process. All digging was done by hand shoveling. Planks were laid on the deep muck. Men lost their boots and shovels and often were mired in muck up to their knees. Horses which became bogged in the muck were often left to die. Surveyors used compasses to find directions in the seven-foot tall marsh grass. The grass was cleared by burning it, and its brilliant glow was seen as far away as Saginaw. Altogether, a two-mile ditch enclosing 400 acres and draining into the Flint River was completed in the scheduled eight years. Schrems received his Concord buggy as a bonus.

This reclaimed land was cultivated, and it proved to be very productive. But it was difficult to get laborers to come to this area, and expenses exceeded the income. In 1900 the land was sold to the Saginaw Realty Company, whose owners were Harry T. and William J. Wickes, Albert M. Marshall, and Samuel G. Higgins. Large-scale farming operations were modernized under Manager Emmet T. Bowen's supervision. Although the Company continued ditching and draining the swamp, it required more sophisticated reclaiming techniques to conquer the annual flooding.

The Owosso Sugar company, owned by Pittsburg capitalists, bought the entire farm on February 22, 1903. A large scale reclamation of the swamp was undertaken. Diking was started beginning at the rivers. Dredges were used to dig the ditches inward and the muck was piled twenty feet high. Roads were laid out on top of the dikes and provided transportation around the farm. The dikes held back the flood waters; the canals and ditches drained the land, making it workable. Each steam-driven pump drained water into the Flint River at a rate of 10,000 gallons per minute. The vast swamp was soon dry. This "Big Prairie Farm was known as the largest farm under cultivation east of the Mississippi River."

Access to this farm was only by two means: an entrance from East Road or by the Mosquito Road from St. Charles. Alicia was located one mile from Mosquito Road and serving as the headquarters for the Owosso Sugar Company, it had a general store, post office, boarding house, dance hall, refreshment parlor, large barns, cattle, tool sheds, eighty workmen's cottages, and a grain elevator. A spur track connected to the Grand Trunk Railroad and brought in lumber and supplies and shipped out produce. Electricity, running water, and telephone service were available. The villages of Pitcarnia and Clausdale each had barns and worker's shanties with a foreman. A large mint distillery was located at Pitcarnia.

Over 7,000 acres were under cultivation in sugar beets, peppermint, corn, and rye. About 350 laborers were needed on this large, well-equipped, modern farm. Until WWI newly-arriving immigrant Slovaks provided some temporary labor until they earned enough money to buy their own farms. The Company then became the first in Michigan

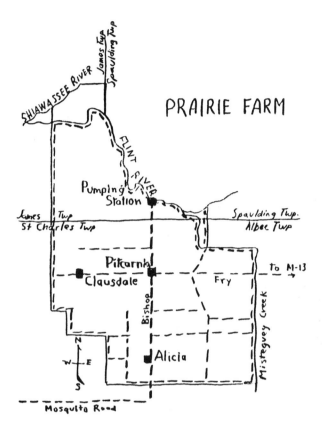

to hire Mexicans to work in the beet fields. Considerable manual labor was required in the sugar beet fields. Experiments with different crops were done. The farm was productive and the owners made profits from the operation.[6]

Holland-born Jacob DeGeus was hired by the Company in 1904. As the farm's general manager he purchased and developed pure-bred Friesan, Holstein, Hereford cattle, Duroc Jersey swine, and Delaine Merino Black Top sheep. The Prairie Farm gained national attention when DeGeus' Belgium Champion draft horses, Garibaldi and Sans

Peur breeds, won top honors in the 1922 New York State Fair. When DeGeus left in 1924 to operate his own farm, the Prairie Farm fell on hard times. The owners tried leasing the farm but eventually sold the farm on June 28, 1933 to the Sunrise Cooperative Farm Community headed by Russian born Jewish immigrant Joseph J. Cohen.

For thirty years Cohen had been involved in reform movements in America. He recruited over one hundred Jewish families from New York slums, totaling about three hundred people who paid $1,000 per family to join the community. These colonists were to live together as one large family in Alicia. The adults lived hotel-like in the large dorm. The children lived together in another large dorm. Both an elementary and high school were established. The group printed their own newspaper. Their motto was *"One for all and all for one."* Their group-elected Executive Board attempted to govern the community.

The group knew nothing about farming and had to hire local farmers to advise and help them. They experimented with vegetable crops but had none for sale. The community had been intended as a self-supporting one without a wage system. Their concept of libertarian anarchism assumed everyone would work together for the benefit of all. This lack of an authoritarian structure resulted in little work motivation, dissension within the ranks, and suspicion of dictatorship. The fourteen families who left the community wrote to the Federal Rural Rehabilitation Corporation. This resulted in further dissension and anger within the community. Under a court injunction the farm was sold December 7, 1936 to the Federal Resettlement Administration.[7]

In the next few years of government ownership , the farm was neglected and used sporadically. The ditches, drainage system and buildings fell into disrepair. On March 1, 1945 the Saginaw Valley

SAGINAW COUNTY FARM LANDS
FOR SALE CHEAP
AND ON EASY TERMS OF PAYMENT.

I have still over 5,000 acres of good Saginaw County Farming Lands for sale. These lands are well located, near good markets, schools and churches, and well watered. Flowing wells can be had at small expense.

I also have lands for sale in Bay, Midland, Clare, Isabella and Gratiot Counties, and City property of all kinds.

If you want to buy or sell Manufacturing Sites, City Property or Farming Land, call on

C. G. FOWLER,

226 North Hamilton Street, Saginaw (West Side).

An 1890 advertisement. Eddy Collection

Cooperative Farms group bought the farm for $265,000 with the intent to divide the farm into individual farms from 320 to 1,000 acre parcels each. On March 10, 1948 the farm was divided into tracts for thirteen individual owners: Ben Albosta, Paul Albosta, Jacob Spindler, Richard Price, Robert Fogg, Edward and Arthur Brabant, Emil Kaiser, Frank Kunick, Frank and Tony Kulhanek, Steve and Walter Wallot. Additional owners have since been added. Over 7,000 acres were cultivated to produce very productive navy and soy beans, sugar beets, wheat, and corn crops. The Prairie Farm continues to be owned and worked by private owners today, proving that the most successful farming is still done by individuals. [8]

By 1890 Saginaw County had 257,818 total acres of farm land with 156,927 acres in improved slashed land. There were 3,332 farms with the average size being 77.38 acres. Leading townships were Birch Run with 247 farms; Blumfield 216; Frankenmuth 231; Tittabawassee 254; Chesaning 197; Bridgeport 193; Buena Vista 176; Saginaw 156; Thomas

Tobias & Caroline Frank on their Auburn, Bay County farm in the 1920's.

142; Maple Grove 169. Previously undeveloped townships had increased their number of farms: Albee with 99; Brady 88; Brant 114; Richland 148; Spaulding 45; St. Charles 90; Swan Creek 66; James 51; Jonesfield 75; Zilwaukee 54; Carrollton 11; Marion 16. Some townships lost farms: Kochville had 102; Taymouth 116. In 1881 the German farming communities of Amelith and Frankenlust were annexed to Bay County as Frankenlust Township.

Saginaw County raised almost 24,000 acres of wheat, selling for 75 cents a bushel, over 29,000 acres of oats, selling for 23 cents a bushel, 13,000 acres of corn selling for 42 cents a bushel, 35,000 acres of hay selling for $8.82 a ton. Livestock had increased to 9,723 horses, 13,079 milch cows, 11,476 other cattle, 9,114 hogs, and 19,989 sheep.[9]

By 1901 the county's farm land increased to 342,584 total acres with 240,136 acres in improved, slashed land. Total farms had increased to 4,632 with 74 acres being the average farm. Steady growth was

Milking time on the Rueger farm in Frankenlust Township in the 1920's.

progressing throughout the county, with an overall increase in farms in almost all townships. The entire county was becoming cleared and put into active agricultural production.

The southern and western townships continued to show the greatest growth. Albee now had 142 farms; Brady 246; Brant 170; Richland 221; Spaulding 75; St. Charles 162; Swan Creek 93; James 68; Jonesfield 122; Marion 127. Zilwaukee decreased to 47 farms, and Carrollton now had 17 farms. Farm land continued being sold and improved in the outlying townships.

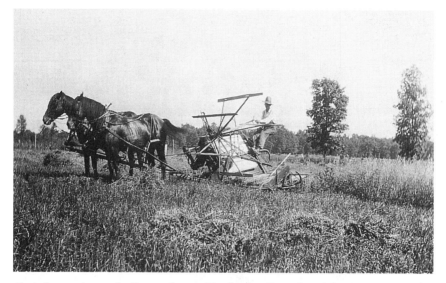

Grain harvesting on the Rueger farm in Frankenlust Township in the 1920's. The grain is cut, then loaded on a wagon and manually forked into a thrasher, then dried and stored in the barn's granaries. The entire family is needed to help.

In 1901, 4,632 county farmers raised almost 29,000 acres of wheat, 31,000 acres of corn, 38,000 acres of oats, 4,745 acres of potatoes, 7,855 acres of beans, and over 49,000 acres of hay. The new sugar beet crop of 1,476 acres produced 17,226 tons of beets. Livestock continued to increase with 12,506 horses, 13,787 other cattle, 17,069 milch cows, 8,469 hogs, and 21,530 sheep.[10]

Saginaw's worthless, mosquito-infested swamp was converted into one of the richest agricultural-producing lands in Michigan. Saginaw County agriculture continued to develop into one of its largest industries and continues to be a thriving industry today as Saginaw has become one of Michigan's leading agricultural producing counties. Farming has become more modern with labor-saving machinery. Continuing experiments have produced new methods of farming, utilizing less acreage, making it more productive, capable of feeding more people

Grain harvesting on the Frank farm in Auburn, Bay County in the early 1930's. This tractor-driven equipment cuts and thrashes the grain simultaneously but the entire family still helps. The grain is manually unloaded into the barn's granaries for drying and storage.

Corn harvesting on the Ederer farm in Thomas Township in October 1998. This modern harvester requires only two men to do the job. While Bill Sparks combines, Joe Sparks drives the loaded grain truck to Carrollton's Countrymark elevator on the Saginaw River for drying and storage. The Great Lakes freighters will eventually move the grain to Maumee, Ohio and then to European ports.

and livestock than ever before.

Agriculture became a way of life for thousands of people. Many second, third, and fourth generations of the same family have continued to farm the same farms their ancestors settled and cleared. Farms became centennial farms in the 1950's and have been designated as such by the Michigan Historical Commission, receiving yard plaques from Consumers Power Company. The same family continues to live on their farm and own at least ten acres or more of the original farm.

Since the 1950's several new farms have been added to the Centennial Farms roster. Others have lost their centennial status when they were sold for new development—subdivisions, shopping malls, expressways, recreational purposes. New centennial farms are added to the roster each year. Currently, Saginaw County has 226 centennial farms, and fifteen of these are 150 years or older. This is indeed an honor to those early settlers who so courageously conquered the wilderness and a testimony to the perseverance of the succeeding generations who continued farming, improving the industry with each generation, helping to make Saginaw County a leader in Michigan's agricultural production today.

FOOTNOTES

1 *History of Saginaw County*, pages 681 – 702

2 *Letters From Michigan Farmers*

3 *Ibid*

4 *Ibid*

5 *First Annual Report of State of Michign*, Farms and Farm Products

6 *The Saginaw Prairie*

7 *Michigan Utopia: The Sunrise Cooperative Farm Community*

8 *Saginaw News*, 3/10/1948

9 *Twenty-Third Annual Report of Secretary of State*

10 *Ibid*

BIBLIOGRAPHY

First Annual Report of State of Michigan, Farms and Farm Products, W.S. George & Co., State Printers & Binders, Lansing, 1878 –1879, 1880 – 1881, 1881 – 1882

LeCureux, Keith, *The Saginaw Prairie*, Standley Publishing Co., Lansing, Michigan

LeMieux, Christina M., *Michigan Utopia: The Sunrise Cooperative Farm Community from Chronicle*, State Historical Commission, Volume 23, No. 6, March – April 1988

Letters from Michigan Farmers, The Flint & Pere Marquette Railway Company, 1878

Mills, James, *History of Saginaw County*, 1918, Volume I, pages 7 – 20, 681 – 702

Saginaw Courier Herald, 5/22/1904

Saginaw Daily News,
7/17/27,
12/20/1935,
7/15, 8/4, and 8/5/1936,
10/20 and 11/15/1944

Saginaw News,
3/10/48,
7/23/52,
5/23/57,
5/27/62

Tenth Annual Report of Secretary of State, Relating to Farms and Farm Products 1887 – 1888, Davis D. Thorp, State Printer & Binder, Lansing, 1889

Twenty-Third Annual Report of Secretary of State, by Fred M. Warner, Secretary of State, Robert Smith & Co., Lansing State Printers, 1889 – 1890, 1900- 1901

VIII MICHIGAN'S SUGAR BOWL

The large European sugar industry had developed and prospered after Napoleon offered a bonus in 1806. Russia became a leading sugar beet producing country. After the Michigan Legislature offered a sugar bounty in 1837, Lucius Lyon built the White Pigeon Sugar Factory in 1839. He planted thirty acres of sugar beets with seeds imported from Germany. His crop was partially destroyed by worms and grasshoppers. His factory had the capacity of producing five tons of beets daily. The molasses produced was inferior. The whole project resulted in an unsuccessful disaster, and the factory was dismantled in 1840.[1]

While Michigan Immigration Agent Max H. Allardt was living in Bavaria, Germany in June 1870 to recruit Bavarians to immigrate to Michigan, he became interested in Germany's large sugar industry. He sent a bushel of sugar beet seed home to Charles L. Ortmann, who later became East Saginaw's mayor. Allardt wanted the seeds introduced in the Saginaw Valley and in Michigan. Ortmann advertised the seeds in the *Courier* and distributed them free of charge to interested farmers. He also sent seed packages to the editors of newspapers in Cheboygan, Grand Traverse, St. Louis, Alpena, Mackinaw, St. Joseph, Monroe, and Detroit. Sugar beet growing was a little understood, new venture, and its promotional efforts proved unsuccessful.

In 1881 the Michigan Legislature again appropriated $1500 for experimentation with sorghum culture by offering a bounty of two cents per pound for sorghum sugar produced. The intent was to bolster a liquid sugar industry.

In 1884 Joseph Seemann visited his birthplace in Bohemia, Austria, an area with one- hundred- thirty-one sugar mills, employing thousands of workers, and he also became interested in the sugar beet industry. When he revisited Bohemia in 1889, he sent Kleinwenzleben sugar beet seeds home to his East Saginaw business partner, Charles H. Peters. He advertised them in their newspaper, the *Saginaw Zeitung,* mailing the seed to any interested person who enclosed his proper address along with a two-cent stamp.[2]

Peters had also forwarded some of the seed to Professor R.C Kedzie of Michigan Agricultural College at Lansing. With the aid of student Edwin C. Peters, Kedzie grew the seeds in an experimental plot in Saginaw County. They learned that the beets could be grown on sandy loam soil. Beet sizes ranged from one to four pounds, producing twelve to thirty-two tons per acre. Seemann returned to Saginaw with a number of German pamphlets on sugar beets and distributed them to farmers. He also published a series of articles on sugar beets in his German newspaper, the *Saginaw Zeitung.* Some German immigrants had already become familiar with the beet industry while they still lived in Germany. Allardt instructed these German-American farmers about this new venture.

Attorney Samuel G. Higgins became interested in a sugar industry and in 1894 he began interesting local businessmen in the industry. In 1897 he combined with Harry T. Wickes, Thomas A. Harvey, and George B. Morley to purchase sugar beet seeds and the John Baxter farm in Spaulding Township. They renamed it the Saginaw Improvement

This Bridgeport Township sugar beet plot in 1895 was one of the first in Saginaw County. This small plot required family and friends to plant, thin, hoe, and harvest. At this time raising sugar beets was still a mystery to farmers. Eddy Collection

Farm and planted several acres of sugar beets. They also encouraged six hundred farmers to plant, thin, and cultivate small plots of beets on their own farms. Mr. Lenders, a chemist knowledgeable in sugar processing, was hired to assist and instruct the farmers.

In October 1897, a vacant store on Genesee & Franklin Streets was used to exhibit five hundred twenty-seven separate sugar beet specimens. These successful experiments attracted additional attention to sugar beet production and prompted Higgins to state: *Three crops of beets produced in consecutive years are worth as much as one crop of pine which grew one hundred years or more.*[3]

In 1895 Senator George A. Prescott concerned about the declining lumber industry had turned his attention to sugar beets as a replacement. Several lawmakers joined him in the same crusade and the Michigan

Legislature passed the Youman's Sugar Bounty Law on March 26, 1897. The Bounty granted one cent per pound to beet processors for Michigan-produced sugar, above ninety per cent purity, providing that farmers received at least four dollars per ton for beets with twelve per cent sugar content. This bounty would be paid for seven years.

The Bay City Businessmen's Association under the direction of N.B. Bradley became the first group to incorporate and establish a sugar factory in October 1897. Bay City businessmen soon pledged $200,000. Many sites were considered but the site selected was the City Council-donated-property in Essexville near the mouth of the Saginaw River.

When the Michigan Sugar Company announced on January 6, 1898 that they would build Michigan's first factory in Essexville, the entire community celebrated. Every home and store was illuminated and bunting was displayed everywhere. One thousand farmers agreed to plant 3,000 acres, and forty pounds of sugar beet seed had been imported from Europe. Frederick W. Wolf began factory construction with machinery manufactured in Germany.

It was a grand day when the Essexville factory opened on October 17, 1898. Farmers brought in thirty-four tons of beets that day. Governor Hazen Pingree visited. This first sugar campaign lasted until February 1899. The plant had the capacity of processing five hundred tons per day. A total of 32,000 tons of beets were processed with 292 tons sliced daily, and five and one-quarter million pounds of white sugar being produced.[4]

The tremendous success of this plant resulted in eight additional plants being built in 1899. Bay City added two additional plants—Bay City Sugar Co. and West Bay City Sugar Co. Other plants were constructed in Rochester, Kalamazoo, Benton Harbor, Holland, Alma, and Caro.

The entire village of Caro turned out on January 31, 1899 when banker Charles Montague announced he had secured financing in Detroit for a new sugar factory. The band played *HAIL TO THE CHIEF* and two hundred young men each carried a pole topped with a sugar beet and a torch. The new factory would be The Peninsular Sugar Refining Company. A one-hundred-acre site was selected on a bluff fifty feet above the Cass River at the foot of Almer Street. The Caro Water Company would contribute 500,000 gallons of spring water daily. Tuscola County farmers agreed to plant their acreage into beets. Caro school boys and girls earned $6 to $9 per week working in the beet fields that summer. The A. Wernicke Maschinenbau Company of Germany constructed the plant with a crew of three hundred men working ten hour shifts. When it was completed, the factory looked like one of the many medieval castles on Germany's Rhine River. The factory and its campaign proved to be very successful that year.[5]

Between 1898 and 1904, twenty-three factories were established in Michigan. The numerous plants were too small, inefficient, and unprofitable. Their close proximity created intense competition. In 1899 beet wagons were lined up extending twenty blocks into Bay City. Mile-long wagons waited at the other Bay City plants. In 1901 the German-American Sugar Company opened up at Salzburg. It later became the Monitor Sugar Company. Bay City was the only community with four sugar factories. With so many competing factories, beet wagons would be hijacked at the city limits. Sitters for each factory sat guard and enticed farmers with bribes, cigars, or physical means to deliver to their respective factory.

The Sugar Bounty Law was to exist until 1904. The Supreme Court

Farmers with their teams and beet wagons were lined up for several city blocks at a sugar factory. They were waiting to unload their wagons. It was a lengthy process since each farmer had to shovel his own beets onto a pile eight feet high. The same scene was repeated at every factory in Bay City, Carrollton, and Caro. Eddy Collection

repealed the Sugar Bounty Law in September 1900 when nineteen factories were operating. The Essexville plant had collected $50,000. Elimination of the bounty created no adverse impact on the steadily developing sugar industry.

Conservative Saginaw businessmen did not organize a factory until 1900. They waited to build their factory taking advantage of mistakes made in other pioneer factory construction. In 1899 several farmers in Spaulding Township grew beets, but with a shortage of railroad cars they had considerable difficulty in getting them to the factory. Many fed their crop to their livestock. Lumberman W.V. Penoyer and several other capitalists organized the Saginaw Sugar Company in 1900 with $500,000 capital. The site selected was the H.P. Smith property at South Jefferson & Sidney (Rust) Streets. There had been great concern about the salt in the Saginaw River water supply and the factory was delayed until confirmation from Washington indicated that it would not adversely affect the beets.

The Kilby Manufacturing Company began construction on the new plant in the summer of 1901. The plant was 240' long x 64' wide and four stories high. The steel framework loomed high above the neighboring trees and was visible for many miles, even to Washington Avenue. It was enclosed in brick walls and filled with complex machinery and Wickes boilers. The beets would be brought to the main building on a long conveyor connecting with the beet sheds. Inside, the beets would then run through a cutting process to convert the pulp into a ribbon-like substance looking like sauerkraut. Then it would be thrown into vats and saturated with water. When the water was drawn off, it would continue through a carbonating and clarifying process. Evaporation would be the next step before sugar crystals appeared.[6]

The main building could store over 10,000 barrels of sugar. An adjacent cooper shop made all shipping barrels. Large quantities of lime manufactured in its own onsite kiln would be used in the clarifying process. One building stored sixty tons of stone to make the lime. The factory would be able to accept six hundred tons of beets a day. There were two railroad switches to the plant. The beet storage sheds held several hundred tons of beets.

When the plant opened in October, beets were delivered all day long to the Saginaw Sugar Company. The beet sheds were always filled with wagons of the continually-arriving farmers. Visitors mulled around the grounds observing this new bustling activity. Farmers hauled their beets in wagons weighing from two to seven tons over macadamized roads in South Saginaw. Since rainy weather did not affect these roads, the farmers could haul in all kinds of fall weather. Some beets were brought into the factory by railroad cars, but there was such a large demand and shortage of these cars that the best, least expensive method for farmers was to haul their own beets by team and wagon.

Up to five hundred tons of beets per day could be processed in this factory, and five hundred barrels of sugar would be produced in a period of thirty hours. In this successful 1901 sugar campaign the company sliced 45,000 tons of beets, manufacturing nine million pounds of granulated sugar. Over 5,300 acres of beets supplied the factory; farmers received a total of $285,000; the total payroll was $50,000; and $60,000 was paid to railroads. Already, 4,600 farmers in Saginaw, Tuscola, Huron, Bay, and Gratiot Counties had signed contracts for the 1902 campaign to produce twice as many beets.

In 1901, thirteen factories were operating in Michigan. Six additional factories were under construction. The thirteen plants had an aggregate daily capacity of 6,650 tons of beets, with each running about ninety days and processing 598,500 tons. Michigan's total sugar produced was 200 million pounds. Each factory used 2,100 tons of lime stone which was obtained from Alpena quarries and 6,752 tons of soft coal which was mined from Saginaw Valley mines. The farmer received about five dollars per ton of beets.[7]

This new sugar industry was proving to be an economic boom to Michigan. About 85,000 people in Michigan helped in growing the beets. Another 27,000 were employed in construction and operation of the factories. Each factory employed about 185 men. Wages averaged about $1.60 per day. Those who worked in factories earned about $2.00 per day. Many types of workers found employment: construction workers, highly skilled mechanics, ordinary day laborers, field workers to weed, thin and harvest the beets. The unemployed found work in this seasonable industry during the sugar campaign's duration from November through February.

Lumbermen with their defunct Saginaw River sawmills now talked eagerly about a promising new Michigan industry. A factory needed to be near a large labor supply source with ample rail and water facilities. The former sawmill locations would be excellent sites. Five rivers emptying into the Saginaw drain a large area suitable for growing sugar beets. Just as they were during lumbering days, these streams could be cleared of obstructions, making them navigable for flat bottom scows. It cost fifty dollars to build a scow that could carry thirty tons of beets. The scows loaded with beets could be brought down the Cass River from Vassar, Frankenmuth and Bridgeport. The Flint River could bring beets from Flushing and other southern points, the Shiawassee from Chesaning, the Bad River from St. Charles, the Tittabawassee from all points along its tributaries to points above Midland. The fertile soil along all these rivers could easily be converted to sugar beet farms. The beet byproducts would be turned into pulp for cattle feed and returned upstream by scows for dairy farmers. The Valley Sugar Company was already building a plant in Carrollton, and the Huron Sugar Company was also considering locating a plant in Saginaw.[8]

The same stockholders in the Saginaw Sugar Company—W. V. Penoyer, H.T. Woodworth, W.A. Baker, W.H. Boutell, Aaron T. Bliss— also organized the Valley Sugar Company in February 1900 with $300,000 capital to be located on Aaron T. Bliss's defunct Carrollton lumber mill site. Kilby Manufacturing Company would also build this factory having a capacity of six hundred tons of beets daily. The beet sheds would be able to handle 25,000 tons of beets. The machinery would be modern and labor saving, and 250 men would be employed to run the factory twenty-four hours per day in twelve hour shifts.

The plant was a little city by itself with its various sugar houses, beet sheds, lime kilns, coal sheds, laboratories, and offices. The five-story main brick building had a steel interior with cement floors. The factory's own power plant furnished its electricity. It manufactured its own lime. Its own machine, tool, and blacksmith shops made all tools and repairs. Every twenty-four hours, the factory used one hundred tons of coal, sixty tons of lime rock, fifteen tons of coke, and four million gallons of water from the Saginaw River. Although 250 employees were hired, all work was done mechanically.[9]

Enthusiasm for this new plant was great. The plant was built in 1902. By March 1902, one thousand farmers had already pledged to raise 6,000 acres. The sugar campaign starting October 20, 1902 was a disappointment because there were barely enough beets to supply both of the Saginaw factories. Six factories within a fifteen-mile radius competed for beets. To encourage greater beet production, Chet Fenton at the Carrollton plant urged farmers to plant fifteen pounds of beet seed per acre and to raise two acres of beets. In 1904 he invited all farmers to come to his Farmers Day convention-exhibition. Fenton displayed beets with placards and cartoons explaining their good and bad characteristics and growing techniques. This was an instructional experience for the 4,000 farmers who came. Farmers Day soon became an anticipated annual event.

In 1903 the Saginaw Sugar Company beset with losses undertook extensive improvements. Modern, efficient machinery which would extract more syrup from the beets was installed. Mistakes made originally in plant construction were now being corrected. This factory was disadvantaged with its site a mile away from its water source, its limited railroad connections, and its limited plant capacity. Water was needed in all processes of sugar making, and extra expenses for piping in water were incurred. In 1905 this plant merged with the Carrollton plant becoming the Saginaw Valley Sugar Company. The machinery from the plant was dismantled and sold to a factory in Sterling, Colorado.

The intensively competitive Michigan sugar plants experienced fierce competition with the Eastern sugar trust which was competing with Western and Midwestern sugar manufacturers. In August 1903, the Saginaw Valley Sugar Company along with several Michigan sugar companies merged with the New York Sugar Trust. In 1903 two Bay City factories merged to form the Bay City-Michigan Sugar Company. On August 20, 1906 six plants in Alma, Caro, Bay City, Sebewaing, Croswell, and Carrollton merged, forming the Michigan Sugar Company. This new merger centralized leadership and encouraged more success in the industry. Michigan Sugar acquired plants in Owosso and Lansing in 1924 and Mt. Pleasant in 1948.[10]

Other factories eventually went out of business or closed during the Great Depression. The German-American plant in Salzburg merged with the Robert Gage Coal Company in 1932 and became the Monitor Sugar Company. It is today the largest sugar beet processing plant in the Eastern United States.

Stiff competition prevailed in the beet industry. The United States Department of Agriculture was experimenting with more productive, disease resistant beet seeds in other beet growing states—Colorado, Utah, California, Oregon, Washington, and Idaho.

In 1910 the Michigan Sugar Company began buying up farms in Saginaw, Alma, Sebewaing, and Huron County and contracting them to Russian families to grow a certain acreage of beets. Russian families

In the late 1920's and 1930's most farmers were using trucks to deliver their beets to the sugar factory. Farmers could now unload their trucks somewhat easier than before, but trucks were still lined up several blocks long waiting for their turn to unload. The piles of beets at any factory looked like a large mountain. Eddy Collection

were large, already experienced in beet growing, and proved to be excellent beet workers.[11]

The Michigan Sugar Company introduced a byproduct for cattle fodder in 1911. Discovered in Germany, it was a mix of molasses and beet pulp. The fodder was palatable, satisfying and made feed more economical and beneficial. New machinery was installed in plants in Alma and Bay City to process this pulp.

In 1932 the sugar companies and beet growers united to form the Farmers & Manufacturers Beet Sugar Association. Both growers and producers could work together to promote, modernize, and expand the industry. Until 1935 the American sugar industry was heavily dependent upon Europe for seeds and machinery. With fewer factories and more efficient methods, greater productivity could be achieved. By the late 1950's only the Monitor Sugar Company and Michigan Sugar Company with factories in Caro, Bay City, Carrollton, Croswell, and Sebewaing remained. Michigan beet growing became centralized in the Saginaw Bay-Thumb area.

The Michigan sugar industry continued to improve, expand, and become more productive with fewer acres. In the period 1910 through 1919, sixteen factories produced 113,000 tons of sugar. Beets were grown in fifty counties on a total of 114,000 acres which produced 940,000 tons of beets. Each acre yielded eight tons of beets. From 1960 through 1974, five factories produced 147,000 tons of sugar. Only nineteen counties raised 79,800 acres for a total of 1,362,000 tons. Since World War II the number of farmers and beet producing counties have continued to decline, but yields continue to increase. Since 1976 there are only five sugar factories in Michigan—Michigan Sugar's plants at Caro, Carrollton, Sebewaing, and Croswell and Monitor Sugar Company in Bay City.

The multigerm beet seed was imported from Germany until 1935. Each seed ball produced six plants which necessitated manually thinning out five plants. The seed was not adapted to American virus diseases and grasshoppers. About fifteen pounds of seed were planted per acre. This produced about 50,000 plants per pound and the plants had to be thinned to 25,000 plants per acre.

Several seed experiments were conducted in the Western United States. First, segmenting the multigerm seed in which seeds were broken apart was practiced. Then decorticating, in which seed was rubbed apart instead of broken into pieces was developed. After World War II

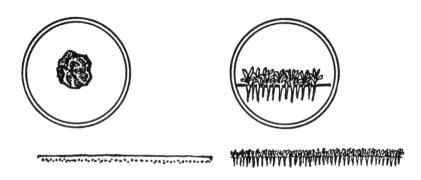

The sugar beet seed of commerce is, in actuality, a "seed-ball" containing a number of germs

The seed is "drilled" in continuous rows The rows are from 18" to 22" apart.

The seedlings appear in solid rows. As soon as the rows can be observed, culti vation begins.

The growing season averages about 170 days.

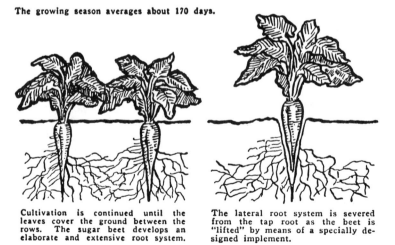

Cultivation is continued until the leaves cover the ground between the rows. The sugar beet develops an elaborate and extensive root system.

The lateral root system is severed from the tap root as the beet is "lifted" by means of a specially designed implement.

When the fourth seedling leaf appears, the rows are "blocked" in such a manner as to leave a cluster of seedlings every 10"

The clusters are "thinned," leaving only one seedling every 10" in the row.

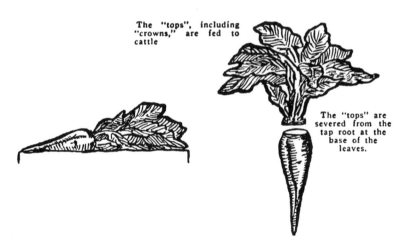

The "tops", including "crowns," are fed to cattle

The "tops" are severed from the tap root at the base of the leaves.

After being lifted, the sugar beets are "pulled" by hand.

A 1933 description of the multigerm beet seed.

the United States Department of Agriculture rescued Drs. V.F. & Helen Savitsky, Russian research scientists, from a displaced persons camp in Western Germany. Both were hired to work for the United States Department of Agriculture to develop a single germ seed for American beet growers. Their new monogerm seed was developed in Oregon, and has been in use in the United States since 1957. This one-plant germination seed has saved countless hours of labor and expense in sugar beet growing.[12]

Originally farmers could only raise about two acres of beets since countless hours of labor were involved. The entire family worked in the fields to thin the beets, then hoe, and cultivate them. A fifteen-acre field was large. Beets were harvested with a team of horses and a puller. Each beet was topped by hand. It generally took four people all day to top one acre of beets. Then the beets were piled in the field to be forked or scooped onto wagons for delivery to the factory. During harvest time, a farmer often would go into town and load his wagon with boys who worked as day laborers to top beets.

Beets were hauled a distance up to twenty-five miles by horse and wagon to a railroad weigh station to be shipped by freight car to a factory. The weigh master was completely in charge at the receiving station, deciding who could deliver beets that day. Farmers were immediately paid cash upon delivery of their beets. Other farmers hauled their beets by teams and wagons and sleighs direct to the factories. A farmer would leave home as early as 5:30 A.M. When he approached the factory and its whistles, his horses became hard to control. He could only travel as fast as his horses would go. A round trip from home to the factory up to twenty-five miles would take all day, since he wouldn't return home until 3:00 P.M. At the factory the farmers had to unload their own

The entire family was involved in topping beets. The beets on this farm are laid out in neat piles waiting to be forked into a truck to be taken to the factory. Eddy Collection

wagons, piling beets eight feet high.

After World War II modern technology was developed for the beet industry. New harvesters simultaneously pulled and topped the beets, shaking off dirt, then loaded them in a truck for delivery to the factory. Sugar beet planters and harvesters continue to be improved making the growing and harvesting of beets more mechanical, eliminating the manual labor so necessary in the industry's early years.

Chemists have been hired to work in sugar factories, solving production problems. Karl Lindfors was chief chemist at Michigan Sugar Company for thirty years. Born in Sweden in 1876, he had learned the sugar industry as chief chemist in Germany. He came to Michigan in 1902 and became the chief chemist at Carrollton in 1904. During his tenure he directed chemical research for all the company's plants

This large mountain of sugar beets is the product from many Valley farmers. It is waiting to be carried into the sugar factory to be processed into sugar. The sugar campaign begins in November and runs until February when these beet piles are moved into the factory and processed. Eddy Collection

helping to streamline the operations, making sugar production more efficient.

Since the industry's inception several methods have been tried to obtain pure sugar, but every factory follows the same procedures. Trucks unload the beets which are piled in air-conditioned storage piles. They are moved into the plant on conveyors. Beets are first washed and cut into long, thin strips or cossettes. Then they enter a diffuser which extracts raw juice and discharges the pulp to a dryer. This raw juice is purified by mixing with a lime recipe. Then evaporators remove the excess water from the juice. The juice is boiled until it is crystallized.

Sugar beets begin their journey into the factory on these automatic conveyors as shown in the Carrollton's Michigan Sugar Factory in October 1998.

This "massecuite" consists of sugar crystals and syrup. In the last boiling stage, the crystals and syrup are separated, then dried. The final product—pure white sugar—is packed in bags for sale. The syrup is reboiled into molasses.[13]

Michigan's sugar industry continues to be a thriving industry today. The Michigan Historical Commission has recognized that the Saginaw-Bay Valley is Michigan's and the Midwest's most important, productive

These sugar beets growing in July 1999 at the Michigan State University's Bean Beet Research Farm in Swan Creek Township are undergoing testing and experiments to improve the sugar beets grown in the Saginaw Valley. Ongoing experiments continue to make the sugar beet industry more productive with each passing year.

beet growing area. In May 1957, a marker was placed in Veterans Memorial Park on the Veterans Memorial Highway at the Bay-Saginaw County line, proclaiming the area as Michigan's Sugar Bowl. In 1976 a second marker was placed at Woodside & Scheurmann Streets in Essexville, marking this site as Michigan's first sugar beet plant. The third marker was placed at Michigan Sugar Company in Caro, proclaiming that factory to be the oldest operating sugar beet factory in the Eastern United States. All three sites remain on the Michigan State Register of Historic Places. Sugar beet production continues today in Saginaw and Bay Counties and the Thumb area. It continues to be more productive with each passing year.[14]

FOOTNOTES

1 *Sweet Success—The Story of Michigan Beet Sugar Industry*

2 *Saginaw Evening News*, 6/12/1889

3 *History of Saginaw County*, page 473

4 *Special Bicentennial Issue of Sugar Beet Journal*

5 *Ibid*

6 *Saginaw Evening News*, 7/13/1901

7 *Saginaw Courier Herald*, 10/15/1901

8 *Ibid*, 9/27/1901

9 *Saginaw Courier Herald*, 2/15/1900

10 *Special Bicentennial Issue of Sugar Beet Journal*

11 *Saginaw Daily News*, 9/27/1910

12 *Special Bicentennial Issue of Sugar Beet Journal*

13 *Ibid*

14 *Ibid and Saginaw News*, 5/12/1957

BIBLIOGRAPHY

Gansser, Augustus H., *History of Bay County Michigan and Representative Citizens*, Richmond & Arnold, Chicago, Illinois, 1905

Henley, Ronald L., Sweet Success—*The Story of Michigan Beet Sugar Industry*, Michigan History Division, Series 3, Number 4, Michigan Industries

Mills, James, *History of Saginaw County*, 1918, Volume I, pages 466 – 487

Saginaw Courier Herald,
2/15/1900, page 7,
9/27/1901, page 5, 10/15, 10/29, and 10/30/1901, pages 8, 6, and 5,
7/12, 8/12, and 8/20/1903, pages 14, 2, and 3,
8/4/1906, page 2,
1/4/1918, pages 1 & 7

Saginaw Daily News,
9/27/1910, page 7,
1/11 and 3/7/11, pages 1 and 5,
3/29/1925,
6/27/1926,
7/21 and 10/11/1932,
6/17/1934,
9/8/1938,
5/22 and 6/30/1946

Saginaw Evening News,
6/12/1889, page 7,
7/13/1901, page 6,
1/13/1908, page 6

Saginaw News,
2/10/1940,
5/12/1957,
10/23/1958

The Bay City Times, 11/22/1998, page 1

Special Bicentennial Issue of Sugar Beet Journal, Summer/Fall 1976, Volume 40, No. 1

IX Saginaw Coal Fields

Saginaw Valley Indians and early settlers had found surface coal on the Tittabawassee, Flint, and Shiawassee Rivers. Blacksmith Stout found surface coal in 1850 on the Shiawassee River bed in Chesaning and used it in his business. Underground coal was first discovered in 1859 when the East Saginaw Salt Manufacturing Company drilled its first salt well on the east bank of the Saginaw River. Two coal bearing strata were found—a 23-foot thick layer at a depth of 211 feet and a ten foot thick layer at a depth of 246 feet. Nothing was done to examine the extent of this coal find. With each salt well bored along the river at various places, drillers pierced veins of black shale. Drillers also had to deal with quicksand and water above the bedrock. But at this time, investors and mill operators sought the salt brine instead of the coal. Timber was plentiful, and it had to be removed and burned to make room for sawmills from which to make fortunes in the developing lumber industry.

Bituminous coal was found in two 164-foot shafts in 1875 on the Shattuck farm on Midland & Shattuck Roads. Soon thereafter, coal was found 158 feet deep on the William Badger farm on the Tittabawassee River. Geologist Dr. Lathrop stated that the entire Valley was threaded with coal. After surveying in 1876, state geologist C. Rominger stated that a rich coal district would be found in the Rifle

River area, covering 8,000 square miles. However, there was no economic reason to manufacture coal until the lumber industry became defunct in the 1890's.

Coal was first discovered in Bay City when William Walker bore a salt well in 1861. He brought a sackful of coal to the Boutell House where it was burned in the stove. This coal discovery created some interest but nothing further developed since timber fuel was still plentiful.

Ira Bennett, a former Pennsylvania coal miner, was living on a farm on the Rifle River in Bay County (now Arenac County) in 1876 when he knew coal was present just by the taste of the water. He dug 25 feet below the river bank and found coal deposits. Bennett took a bagful to the Culver lumber camp. The Eureka Coal Company was then organized by Bay City capitalists with L.L. Culver as president. This was the first company to mine coal in the Saginaw Valley. A 30-foot deep shaft was roomed out in various directions and the land was terraced. An eight feet coal vein was located. About 200 tons were mined and sent to various places in Michigan. The mine was soon abandoned when the Michigan Central Railroad Company would not run its line to the mine unless 200 tons would be mined daily. There was no market for this large tonnage of coal.[1]

Well borer John Russell discovered coal in a four foot vein in Sebewaing in 1889. He reported this to William L. Webber in Saginaw, who then organized the Saginaw Bay Coal Company. Mining was commenced in 1890 and the coal was shipped by the Saginaw, Tuscola & Huron Railroad to Saginaw, Flint, Bay City, and other localities. This mine was closed in 1894, but the Sebewaing Coal Company was organized a few years later and mined successfully for several years.

The first successful Saginaw County mine was located   by four employees of the Street Railway Company—Frederick Brueck, Jr., Joseph Partridge, Alex Bradley, and John Harrison—in Albee Township in 1894. This Verne Mine was located more than three miles from the Grand Trunk Railroad and twelve miles south of Saginaw. Its coal was sold and hauled by wagon to nearby farmers and villages. In 1897 the Verne Coal Company with W.T. Chappel as president purchased the mine for $25,000. A spur track from the mine to the railroad was built along with a company town of twenty cottages, boarding houses, hotel, and store. By 1899, the mine employed 125 men mining 300 tons of good-quality, smokeless coal daily. Over 2,000 acres of land were under lease. Miners from West Virginia were brought here to work in the mine and live in the company town.[2]

The Saginaw Coal Company was incorporated and began mining in October 1896 with $75,000 capital and W.T. Chappell as president in Buena Vista Township on the site of the present-day Saginaw High School. There were private switches to the Flint & Pere Marquette and Grand Trunk Railroads. The 165 foot deep shaft had a 42 inch thick coal vein. Its bright, clean coal was burned in open grates. The company controlled 600 acres, producing 3,000 tons per acre. By 1899, 250 men were employed for $2.00 per day, producing 800 tons of coal daily. The company was one of Saginaw County's most productive mines. It was abandoned in 1913 when it became unprofitable to mine its extended coal veins.

A description of the Crow Island Coal Mine in June 1898 was also a similar description of those early coal mines in the Saginaw-Bay Valley. "LEROY's!" shouted the brakeman as the train with its fifteen miners slowed up in the middle of the desolate marsh in front of a couple rough looking, unpretentious wooden structures of the Crow Island

This Saginaw Coal Company was on the site of Bates Park, the present-day Saginaw High School, when this photo was taken on August 15, 1896. The men have donned their miners' clothes and are ready to descend into the underground mine through the shaft's opening. The coal was brought above ground through the same opening. Plant superintendent John Snowball is on the far left. Eddy Collection

Mine. The signal post for the train stop read "LEROY'S". Harry E. LeRoy had drilled the shaft and now was the plant superintendent. The tall block tower was built immediately over the shaft; the adjoining shelter housed the hoisting engine. Heaps of sand and crumbled rock were thrown about the opening and around the coal and fuel sheds. A desolate stretch of marsh reached to the river bank on one side of the mine. Fields of the Saginaw Lumber & Salt Co. stretched endlessly on the opposite side. In the distance the spires of the two Saginaw cities dotted the landscape. Scattered along the river bank were towers of the abandoned salt wells. A short distance away was the abandoned test hole and rusting field engine where Wills Creek Company had drilled unsuccessfully for a coal mine.

The gaping mine shaft was a mere black hole with an iron shaft that reached 100 feet down, and rock was punctured fifteen feet beyond that. After staring down the hole and becoming accustomed to the darkness, one could see twinkling lights from the miners' hats in its depths. Human sounds came echoing up the hollow hole like thunder. After donning their miners' oilcloth suits, the men were lowered in buckets to the bottom of the shaft by the steam pipe, a cast iron pipe with eight sections each weighing 12,000 pounds and firmly cemented together with 300 pounds of lead. At the end was the "shoe" which rested on a solid sandstone foundation caulked with oakum and Portland cement.

The men filled their cars with the loosened rock and sand which explosives the previous day had made possible. The loaded cars were then pulled to the mouth of the shaft by gravity and the rope system from the engines. The empty cars were pulled down into the mine on another track. This process was repeated throughout the work day. Circular coal pillars were left to support the roof underground. At the end of the work day the mine was readied for overnight explosives to loosen coal for the following day. Each succeeding coal vein would be thicker and harder than the previous one. Crow Island's first vein was located at 275 feet. The veins sloped upward, giving the appearance of hills and valleys. The Crow Island Mine had 1,000 acres under lease.[3]

Bay County's coal mining also began in 1893 when coal was discovered while boring a water well in Monitor Township. In 1895 the Monitor Coal Company was organized and began mining. The Bay Coal Mining Company was organized in 1896. The North American

Chemical Company from England purchased this mine and invested heavily in Bay City, leasing 9,000 acres of land. With their extensive capital, the company could enlarge and modernize its coal mines. Other successful Bay City mines were the Michigan Coal Mining Company in Monitor Township, Oaatka Beach Mine, and the West Bay City Coal Company in Frankenlust Township. This mine revitalized the German Lutheran Amelith colony, prompting new growth and a village and post office to be built. The parochial school was expanded to accommodate the public school.[4]

Saginaw's coal boom brought promoters, speculators, and operators from Ohio, Pennsylvania, West Virginia, and Illinois. Farm land previously selling from $6 to $60 per acre now was selling for $20 to $125 per acre. Over 50,000 Saginaw County acres were leased with land owners receiving from four to eight cents per ton mined. The average company controlled 3,000 acres with each acre producing an average of 3,000 tons valued about $240. Mining companies would secure rights-of-way and provide the grading and ties while railroads would furnish and lay the rails. New jobs were available for laborers and mine bosses; wages ranged from $1.63 to $2.75 per day. Half of these new coal workers were newly-arrived foreign born immigrants. [5]

Coal was already being mined in Corunna, Jackson, and Sebewaing. Saginaw Valley coal deposits were found in St. Charles, Swan Creek, Blumfield, Monitor, Bangor, and Frankenlust Townships. The Valley was threaded with coal. Saginaw's coal burned without cinders or clinkers and contained very little sulphur and iron. It was the best Michigan grade of coal. Former sawmill operators thought that the coal industry would be as prosperous as the lumber industry and that mine shafts would line the river banks as sawmills once had. Already coal was being used in many local manufacturing businesses and the interurbans. It was expected that coal would revive the salt industry and bring various new manufacturing industries such as pottery, fire-brick, sewer pipe, and paving brick to the Valley.

Since the Saginaw Valley had no experienced coal miners, company agents such as the Saginaw Coal Company's Frank S. Spencer recruited unemployed, experienced miners from coal fields in Ohio, West Virginia, and Pennsylvania. Coal mining occurred during the winter months in Michigan, so agents had much difficulty in recruiting unemployed workers for seasonal employment. Traveling in company chartered cars, these recruits often deserted the train at every stop. Most of the coal recruits who did come worked temporarily in Saginaw but left with the lure of higher wages or easier working conditions in the heavy coal mining states. These uneducated transients lived in unkempt little company houses, and created labor problems for mine operators. These recruits never established permanent roots in Michigan. There was always a demand for experienced miners in all mines. Mines were never employed to capacity, as experienced miners changed jobs frequently, and maximum tonnage was seldom achieved.

With the discovery of rich coal veins in St. Charles in 1896, out-of-state mining companies brought the latest equipment. Emerging coal mines revitalized St. Charles, which had almost become extinct with its defunct sawmills. By 1900, St. Charles had over sixty houses, a two-story school, no vacant buildings, and streets lighted with electricity. Many experienced miners from Ohio, Pennsylvania, West Virginia, Tennessee, and Kentucky immigrated to the area. Also, many foreign-born immigrants from Italy, Czechoslovakia, Poland, and Russia came permanently. This new melting pot consisted of a diversity of people.

Some were illiterate, others very educated; some were family men; others were wilder than the former shanty boys. St. Charles became known as "Little Italy" with its social life centering around St. Mary's Catholic Church and its Polish priest.[6]

The J. H. Somers Coal Company of Cleveland invested $45,000 in a mining shaft in St. Charles in November 1897. The shaft was 182 feet deep with a 44 inch coal vein. The company installed electrical machinery and had a direct connection to Michigan Central Railroad. Frank C. Benham was plant superintendent. Mining began in April 1898. The company controlled 2500 acres, employed 300 men at $2.00 per day, and mined 1500 tons of coal daily. J. H. Somers remained one of the largest and first class mining companies in St. Charles. The company eventually leased 5,000 acres and operated three St. Charles mines: #1, the largest, employed 280 men; #2 employed 35 to 100 men; #3 had the richest coal vein. All shafts were 180 feet deep with four foot veins.

Robert Gage and Charles Coryell established the Robert Gage Coal Company in St. Charles in June 1900, controlling 2,000 acres. The company employed 200 men, mining 500 tons daily. In 1907 the company established two salt blocks with its two mining shafts, utilizing the exhaust steam from the engines to produce 400 barrels of salt daily. The Robert Gage Company eventually purchased the J.H. Somers mines.

Coal mines emerged throughout Saginaw County. The Pere Marquette Company started its shaft in 1897 with a $100,000 investment. H.C. Potter, Jr. was president. Its #1 mine was located on the Colelough farm, one mile south of Saginaw. It employed 135 men, mining 800 tons per day. Its #2 mine was located on Gratiot-Brockway Road and employed 35 men. In 1902, the #2 mine was the largest mine in Michigan. The #1 shaft closed in April 1901. [7]

The Standard Mine Company began June 1898 on the Cass Sutherland farm in Bridgeport. Robert Gage was president and A.D. Eddy vice-president. A 140-foot shaft with a 48 inch vein was bored. Modern hoisting and mining engines were installed. There was a direct connection to the Chicago & Grand Trunk Railroad. Over 600 tons of a superior, high-quality coal was mined daily. This mine was a large one, employing from 80 to 90 men.

The James W. Ellsworth Co. began August 1898 in James Township with a 180-foot shaft. This Jimtown mine had direct connections to the Michigan Central Railroad. The company later bought the Willis Creek Co. in St. Charles. The new company became the Northern Coal & Transport and leased 30,000 acres from 600 farms.

Other well-known mines in South Saginaw were the Chappell-Fordney on South Michigan, the Barnard, and the Riverside. Riverside was in the Green Point area and was considered one of the most modern and best equipped in the state. Its coal vein was 30 inches. Men spent their eight hours in the mine, lying on their sides, stomachs, or backs or resting on their knees. The 100 men mined 400 tons of coal daily. These workers lived elsewhere in the city and drove their own autos to work. Their pay averaged about fifty dollars per week. The underground air was always laden with fine coal dust and there was a heavy earthy smell. Both trains and mules were used underground in this mine. Flooding was always a problem at this mine. During the flood in March 1903, the countryside on either side of the Saginaw River was one vast lake. Bridges were damaged and roads in all directions were bottomless. The mine mules were brought above ground. The miners heroically tried to keep the mine from flooding, but the water gained on the pumping

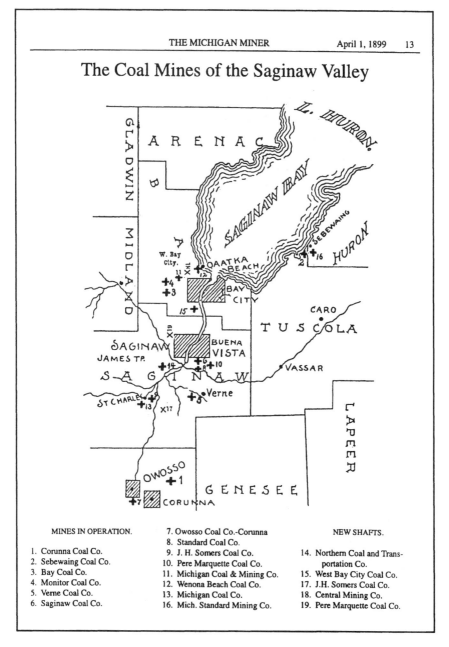

THE MICHIGAN MINER   April 1, 1899   13

The Coal Mines of the Saginaw Valley

MINES IN OPERATION.	7. Owosso Coal Co.-Corunna	NEW SHAFTS.
	8. Standard Coal Co.	
1. Corunna Coal Co.	9. J. H. Somers Coal Co.	14. Northern Coal and Trans-
2. Sebewaing Coal Co.	10. Pere Marquette Coal Co.	portation Co.
3. Bay Coal Co.	11. Michigan Coal & Mining Co.	15. West Bay City Coal Co.
4. Monitor Coal Co.	12. Wenona Beach Coal Co.	17. J.H. Somers Coal Co.
5. Verne Coal Co.	13. Michigan Coal Co.	18. Central Mining Co.
6. Saginaw Coal Co.	16. Mich. Standard Mining Co.	19. Pere Marquette Coal Co.

This map as of April 1, 1899 shows the early mines in the area. Eddy Collection

The Aaron Bliss—Arthur Barnard Mine in James Township in 1905

system. The entire surrounding area looked like a miniature panorama of Venice. The underground Riverside mine also became flooded and was vacated.[8]

Every coal mine was built in the same manner. The tipple was the tall shed built over the shaft's opening. Miners went underground in cages under the tipple, and the same cages were used to bring the coal to the surface.   Other buildings housed the office, the air fan, electric generator, and wash room where the miners changed into mining clothes before descending into the mines. Each miner carried his own carbide lamp, pick, shovel, and lunch pail. He remained underground until the end of the work day. At the end of the day all miners changed into their own clothes after showering with twelve-quart buckets of hot water. Their mining clothes were hung over steam pipes to dry for the following day.

Another world existed in this deep underground coal mine. The subterranean city, cut through clay and coal roofed with slate, was laid

The coal miners have loaded their small rail car in this underground coal mine. The coal will be moved above ground in cages. Eddy Collection

out with intersecting streets, honeycombing several acres of land. All streets led into individual rooms which were the miners' workstations for the day. Coal was mined with "Room & Pillar" method. Pillars of coal, instead of the scarce, expensive timber, were left to support roofs in each individual room assigned to a miner. Each miner spent the day in his room, breaking up the coal chunks he blasted the previous night, loading them into a small rail car. He placed his check or hook in the car which was then pulled through the streets by a driver and a patient, melancholy little mule to the elevator shaft.

The cars were taken above ground in the cages. There a company man and a union man were present while the coal was dumped into a screen, separating the lumps and slack. The miner was generally paid from forty to seventy cents per ton only for the coal lumps. The waste

Melancholy, patient little mules were used extensively in under ground coal mines, living in the mines twenty-four hours per day. At the end of the men's workday, the mules were fed and bedded in their underground stables. Eddy Collection

slack was dumped onto a shale pile. About four P.M. each day, every miner readied his room with dynamite. Each miner learned how to place the fuses so that his coal would result in medium-sized chunks with minimal shale. When every miner simultaneously set off his fuses, the earth shook violently, filling the entire subterranean city with choking dust, making the mine inhabitable for hours. While the men left the mine, the mules were fed and bedded in their underground stables. The dust settled throughout the night so that when the men returned the following day, they retrieved their coal chunks loosened from the previous day's explosions.[9]

Above ground, the coal was weighed so that the miners' wages could be determined. Then it was dumped into a chute inside the tipple. From there it passed over several screens and was graded into different sizes. The slag, coal dust, and sulphur were moved to the shale pile. Sometimes these piles caught fire from the internal combustion. Special machines were then used to wash the impurities and sulphur from the coal. Then the lumps were graded by sizes—buckwheat, pea, chestnut, egg, stove, furnace, and lump coal. The coal was moved into chutes which loaded directly into the railroad cars. The coal was then transported to Saginaw and other outlying points.

Coal mining was highly organized, and all workers had different names and duties. Trappers opened doors for mules; mule skinners drove the mules and cars; miners picked the coal; motor men ran engines; cagers pushed cars; greasers maintained the cars; track layers laid the track; there were timer men and trip riders; weigh masters or company men weighed the coal; check weighmen or union men checked the weigh masters figures. Coal mine workers were all unionized.[10]

Mules, often blinded from their lifetime underground, were only brought above ground during strikes or floods. The early or smaller mines depended on mules to transport the 2,000 pound cars from the miner's room to the cage and return. All work was done manually by the miners. Larger companies with more invested capital installed modern mining machinery and electricity. The loaded cars were moved by electric trolley lines. Work was easier for the miners. Because of the height of the rooms, miners worked kneeling over, on their knees, or

These coal miners are about to descend into the mine. They have donned their fresh miners' clothes, have their lights on their caps, and are carrying their metal lunch pails. They will remain underground until the end of the workday.
Eddy Collection

sides to loosen the coal.

Every miner found his way underground by the light of his open lard-oil lamp hanging like a teapot from his cap. Every mine had some form of gas. There was fire damp, the carbureted hydrogen gas, coming from coal pores. There was black damp, the carbonic acid gas, coming from burning lamps. There was white damp, the sulphuratred hydrogen, coming from powders and explosives. Explosions were minimal since all Saginaw mines had waterlog problems. Often mines were abandoned when they became overrun with water and quicksand. Saginaw mines averaged about twenty annual cave-in accidents involving serious injuries or death. Whenever an accident occurred, whistles were blown. Everyone stopped working. Wives hurried to the mine to learn about the casualty.

In 1897 each mine employed an average of 40 men, who worked an eight or nine hour shift, 159 days per year, with an average daily pay of $2.00. Each miner produced about seven tons daily. By 1900 wages averaged up to $3.00 per day. Married men paid $1.00 per month, single men 50 cents per month, for complete medical-surgical coverage with the company paying all medical costs. Half of the Saginaw miners were foreign born, with an average age of 32 years. In 1903, eleven Saginaw mines employed 1500 men. Average wages of $2.40 per day in 1906 increased to $3.24 per day in 1907. Mine workers worked nine months during winter months when there was a market for coal. Every company had a cluster of one-story-five- room cottages which were rented for $4 to $6 per month to the worker and his family. Miners were paid in cash bi-weekly. There were very few company stores since their absence saved miners money. Most men lived in the cities and commuted to the mines by trains. Workers either drove their own autos or used street cars to commute to city coal mines.[11]

Fluctuating wages and hazardous work conditions resulted in frequent strikes. The longest five-month strike occurred in 1902 when only 869,228 tons were mined compared to 1,004,040 tons in 1901. To continue steady employment, 500 miners contributing a total of $250,000 and their labor, organized the Caledonia Coal Company on September 1, 1905. The company operated continuously through the 1906 strikes when every Michigan mine was shut down. There was no reason to strike since the workers were the owners. The company undersold coal at $3.50 per ton, establishing a Saginaw monopoly, then raised prices to $4.50 per ton where it remained for years. Caledonia went bankrupt in 1916, and Robert Gage bought the assets.

Saginaw's low-sulphur coal was the best in Michigan. However, the coal was found only in narrow, short strips or veins. These three-foot coal veins were never large enough for the modern coal machinery used in West Virginia and Kentucky whose better-quality coal was mined from thicker veins. These states produced coal at lower costs than Saginaw's average of $1.64 per ton production costs. These states began dumping their surplus coal in Saginaw in 1908. As a result many local companies were forced into bankruptcy.

The Consolidated Coal Company was organized February 8, 1906 by Harry T. and William J. Wickes, and Walter S. and Arthur D. Eddy. In 1906 there were sixteen mines in Saginaw. Consolidated owned ten of them—Uncle Henry, Standard Mine #5, Saginaw Old Mine, PM #2, Riverside, Fordney, Cass River, Barnard, Northern Transportation, and Shiawasee. The other six mines were Robert Gage, Somers #1, #2, #3, Caledonia Mine, and Consumers Developing Coal Co. In 1907 Consolidated owned twelve Saginaw mines and additional mines in Bay County. The company unified coal mining while almost gaining a Saginaw monopoly.

Saginaw's coal peak was reached in 1907 when 1,047,927 tons were produced. There were seventeen mines in Saginaw County. Some mines were still utilizing from four to fourteen mules. The Fordney Mine used eight mules; Saginaw Old Mine eleven mules. After this there was a gradual decline with only 584,648 tons mined in 1914. In 1913 there were 39 operating mines in Saginaw and Bay Counties, and eleven mines elsewhere in the state. Of Michigan's total 3,000 miners, 1,500 lived in

This Swan Creek Mining Company was the last operating mine in Saginaw County. When it closed on February 17, 1952, the mining industry met its demise. Eddy Collection

Saginaw County. Robert Gage's No. 8 mine was sunk in 1917 and operated until 1931, the longest period of any Michigan mine. Today this abandoned mine is located on the Hartley Outdoor Education Center.

Saginaw mines were never able to utilize full tonnage because of unreliable drillings, unprofitable strip mining, lack of experienced miners, frequent labor strikes, and insufficient railroad cars to meet maximum capacity production needs. There was a sharp downturn in mining in 1923. Only six mines remained in 1931. Over 700 miners were unemployed by 1936. Gradually all the mines were forced to close. The Swan Creek Mining Company was Saginaw's last operating mine. Its owners reduced the work week to three days because of lack of business.

Coal heat was being replaced with oil and natural gas heating. When this mine closed permanently on February 17, 1952, the Saginaw coal industry met its demise.[12]

Reddish slag heaps such as St. Charles' Garfield shale hill, remained in sugar beet fields and scrub oak woods for years as a reminder of the coal era. Eventually the red-black shale was used on country secondary roads, driveways, and farm lanes. Today coal still lies threaded underground in narrow veins in the Saginaw Valley. The old mining shafts have been closed. Much activity occurs above ground over these old mining sites, with many people unaware that coal mines ever existed far below ground or in Saginaw. Only No. 8 at St. Charles' Hartley Outdoor Education Center can attest to that thriving industry so long ago. A museum has been built to honor those old coal miners and preserve remnants of the past.

FOOTNOTES

1 *The Michigan Miner*

2 *The Coal Fields of Saginaw Michigan*

3 *Saginaw Courier Herald*, 6/5/1898

4 *The Michigan Miner*

5 *Michigan Bureau of Labor & Industrial Statistics*

6 *Ibid*

7 *Ibid*

8 *Saginaw Courier Herald*, 3/12/1903

9 *The Coal Fields of Saginaw Michigan*

10 *History of No. 8 Coal Mine*

11 *Michigan Bureau of Labor & Industrial Statistics*

12 *Saginaw News*, 2/17/1952

BIBLIOGRAPHY

History of No. 8 Coal Mine compiled by Bruce P. Beerbower Affiliate Graduate Student Central Michigan University for Saginaw Intermediate School District

Michigan Bureau of Labor & Industrial Statistics, Annual Reports, Robert Smith Printing Co., Lansing, Michigan, 1897, 1898, 1899, 1900, 1901, 1902, 1903, 1904, 1906, 1907

Mills, James, *History of Saginaw County, Michigan*, Volume I, 1918, pages 447 – 465

Saginaw News,
6/22 and 12/1/1946,
8/24/1947,
2/17/1952,
2/28/1954,
3/7/1965,
7/1/1973,
4/3 and 7/27/1977

Saginaw Courier Herald,
1/7/1894, page 5, c. 1,
4/13/1898, page 5,
5/27/1898, page 7,
6/5/1898, page 10,
3/12/1903, page 5

The Coal Fields of Saginaw Michigan, Chas. B. Schaefer, Publisher, May 1898

The Michigan Miner, The Coal Mines of the Saginaw Valley, December 1, 1898, April 1, 1899